Key Rec...

To identify the aircraft type refer... by checking against the le...

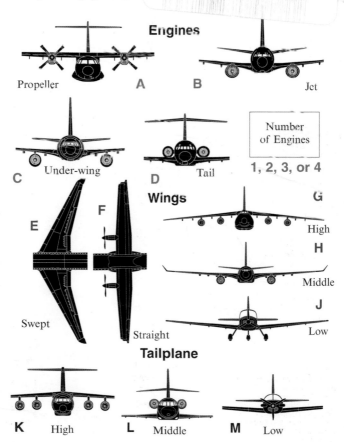

Engines

Propeller   **A**   **B**   Jet

C Under-wing   **D** Tail

Number of Engines

1, 2, 3, or 4

E Swept   **F** Straight

Wings

G High

H Middle

J Low

Tailplane

K High   **L** Middle   **M** Low

Contents

Adam M-309 CarbonAero   *USA*

The M-309 was designed by Burt Rutan as a high performance business and personal aircraft. Of carbon-composite construction it is a pressurised six-seater with a low wing, twin booms, a high-set 'bridge' tailplane and retractable tricycle undercarriage. Its turbocharged TSIO-550 engines are mounted in the nose and rear fuselage. They are fitted with FADEC and the M-309 incorporates the latest developments in glass cockpit technology. The M-309 prototype made its first flight in March 2000. It has been named CarbonAero and some 24 had been ordered by late 2001.

Powerplant: two 261-kW (350-hp) Teledyne Continental TSIO-550 piston engines

Performance: max speed 463 km/h (288 mph), cruising speed 408 km/h (253 mph), initial climb rate 518 m (1,700 ft) per min, range 2760 km (1,725 miles)

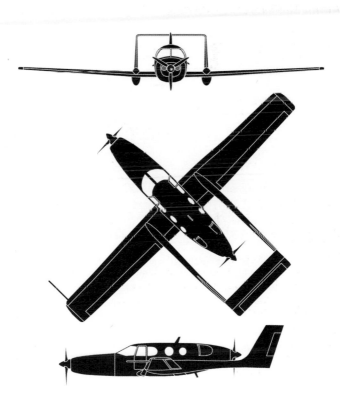

Dimensions: wing span 12.80 m (42 ft), length 10.52 m (34 ft 6 in), height 2.90 m (9 ft 6 in)

Recognition features
A Twin tail booms
B High-set, 'bridge' tailplane
C 'Push-pull' engines

Aérospatiale/BAC Concorde

France/UK

The Concorde supersonic transport was developed under a 1962 British/French agreement by BAC, Sud Aviation, Rolls-Royce and SNECMA. Almost every aspect of the aircraft was revolutionary and the design included a complex ogival delta wing, a drooping nose to give improved vision for take off and landing and four Olympus turbojets mounted in twin fairings under the wings. The cabin was configured for 100 first-class passengers. The first of two prototype, two production prototype and three pre-production (Model 100) aircraft flew on 2 March 1969. Just 13 production aircraft were built, designated Model 101 (French built for Air France) and Model 102 (British built for British Airways). Concorde went into service in January 1976 and 12 were in operation at the time of their grounding on 15 August 2000 following the Paris disaster. After fuel-tank and other modifications, the aircraft returned to transatlantic service on 9 November 2001.

Powerplant: four 169.27-kN (38,050-lb st) Rolls-Royce/SNECMA Olympus 593 Mk 602 afterburning turbojets

Performance: max speed 2180 km/h (1,354 mph), cruising speed 1930 km/h (1,205 mph) range 6300 km (3,938 miles)

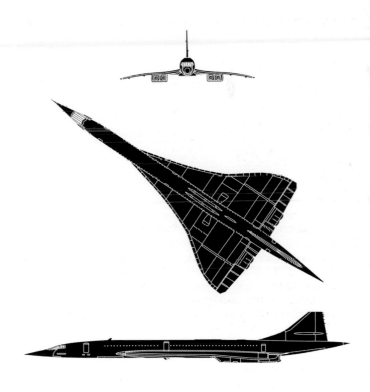

Dimensions: wing span 25.60 m (83 ft 10 in), length 62.10 m (203 ft 9 in), height 11.30 m (37 ft 1 in)

Recognition features
A Long, narrow, needle-like fuselage
B Delta wings
C Broad-chord fin

Air Tractor

The initial AT-300 agplane was designed by Leland Snow. It had a chemical hopper mounted between the single-seat cockpit and the engine firewall. It was fitted with a P&W R-985 radial piston engine and first flew in 1973. Later versions included the AT-301 and AT-302 (Lycoming LTP101 turboprop). Air Tractor then developed variants with larger airframes and with various combinations of hopper size and, generally, turboprops. These included the AT-400 with a slimmer fuselage and larger wing, the AT-400A, and the AT-402 based on the AT-400 with a longer-span wing. The AT-501 is a larger two-seat variant with an R-1340-S3H1-G radial and the equivalent turboprop is the AT-502 (PT6A-15AG). The largest Air Tractors are the two-seat AT-802 which is optimised for crop spraying or fire bombing, and the single-seat AT-802A (above), which is normally powered by a PT6A-67AG.

AT-502
Powerplant: one 507-kW (680-shp) Pratt & Whitney Canada PT6A-15AG turboprop

Performance: max speed 290 km/h (180 mph), cruising speed 253 km/h (157 mph), range 800 km (500 miles)

8

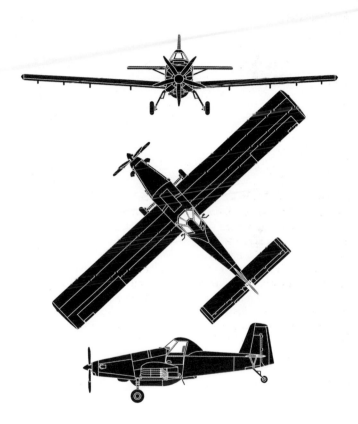

Dimensions: wing span 15.24 m
(50 ft), length 9.90 m (32 ft 6 in),
height 2.99 m (9 ft 9 in)

Recognition features
A Low wing
B Fixed tailwheel U/C
C Prominent enclosed cockpit
D Tall vertical tail

Airbus A310

After the successful launch of the A300, Airbus Industrie produced a new smaller-capacity short/ medium-haul version, the A310. Using a shortened A300 fuselage, the A310 has a smaller wing which is, essentially, a new design. This resulted in an aircraft with 280-passenger capacity, powered by JT9D-7 or General Electric CF6-80 engines. The A310 prototype first flew on 3 April 1982. The basic passenger version is the A310-200, the first of which were delivered to Lufthansa and Swissair in March 1983. The A310-300 (above) is an extended-range variant with extra tailplane fuel tanks and computerised fuel management and approval for North Atlantic ETOPS operations. Some 260 A310s had been ordered by the end of November 2001, with 246 in operation. In military service the A310 flies with Belgium, Canada as the CC-150 Polaris, France and Germany.

A310-200
Powerplant: two 213.50-kN (48,000-lb st) Pratt & Whitney JT9D-7R4D1 turbofans

Performance: cruising speed 973 km/h (608 mph), take-off field length 1860 m (6,100 ft), landing field length 1960 m (6,430 ft), range 6759 km (4,224 miles)

Dimensions: wing span 43.89 m
(144 ft), length 46.66 m (153 ft 1
in), height 15.80 m (51 ft 10 in)

Recognition features
A Short, wide-body fuselage
B Wingtip fences on some aircraft
C Prominent flap-track fairings

Airbus A319/A320/A321 *International*

To compete with the short-haul 737 and DC-9, Airbus launched the A320 in 1980. It is a conventional low-wing aircraft with up to 180 passenger seats and FBW control systems. The cockpit was designed from the outset with a six-screen EFIS and side sticks in place of the conventional control column. The first CFM56-powered A320-111 flew on 22 February 1987 with the first delivery to Air France in March 1988. The A320-200 is the standard, longer-range, version with wingtip fences. The A319, which first flew on 28 August 1995, is a maximum 145-seat version with a shorter fuselage and the A321 which made its maiden flight on 12 December 1996 has a fuselage stretch to carry 220 passengers. The A321-200 is the standard, long-range, version. All members of the A320/319/321 family can be specified with IAE V2500 turbofans. The 107-seat, P&W PW6000-powered, A318 is due to fly in 2002.

A320-200
Powerplant: (typical) two 117.90-kN (26,500-lb st) CFM International CFM56-5A3 turbofans

Performance: cruising speed 949 km/h (593 mph), take-off field length 2336 m (7,665 ft), range 5000 km (3,125 miles)

Dimensions: wing span 33.90 m (111 ft 3 in), length 37.57 m (123 ft 3 in), height 11.80 m (38 ft 8 in)

Recognition features
A Narrow-body fuselage and narrow-chord wings
B Large wing root fairings
C Prominent flap-track fairings

Airbus A330

The long-range market dominated by Boeing with the 747 and the 767-300 was addressed by Airbus with the A330/A340 design. Based on the A300 with a 10-m (32 ft 10 in) fuselage stretch, FBW systems, an EFIS cockpit and a redesigned wing with winglets, the new aircraft was offered with either two engines (Rolls-Royce Trent, Pratt & Whitney PW4000 or GE CF6) as the A330 or with four engines as the A340. Maximum A330-300 capacity is 440 passengers but a short-fuselage A330-200 (above) carries 406 passengers. The A330 prototype flew on 2 November 1992. Major airlines using the A330 include Thai Airways International, Cathay Pacific, LTU, Malaysian, Garuda and Korean Air. A total of 413 A330s had been ordered by late November 2001, with 207 having been delivered and 204 in service.

A330-300
Powerplant: (typical) two 300-kN (67,500-lb st) class General Electric CF6-80E1A4 turbofans

Performance: typical operating Mach No. 0.82, take-off field length 2514 m (8,250 ft), range at 230000 kg (507,050 lb) 10371 km (6,444 miles)

Dimensions: wing span 60.30 m
(197 ft 10 in), length 63.68 m
(208 ft 11 in), height 16.84 m
(55 ft 3 in)

Recognition features
A Only twin-engined wide-body
with winglets
B Winglets
C Large nose radome
D Four-wheel main U/C

Airbus A340

Sharing a common airframe with the A330, the A340 was in fact flown first, in A340-200 form, on 25 October 1991. It differs primarily from the A330 in being powered by four engines (CFM56 as standard, but with the Rolls-Royce Trent available on the A340-500/600) and is therefore suitable for very long-range, over-water flights, being free from ETOPS restrictions. The A340-200, with 420 passenger capacity, has a shorter fuselage but longer range than the A330, while the A340-300 (above) has a small stretch to accommodate an extra 20 passengers. The A340-500/600 are new stretched versions for 440 passengers, the A340-500 also offering ultra-long range. By late November 2001 some 309 A340s of all versions had been ordered, with 209 delivered and operators include Lufthansa and Virgin Atlantic Airways.

A340-200
Powerplant: four 144.60-kN (32,500-lb st) CFM International CFM56-5C3 turbofans

Performance: cruising speed 999 km/h (624 mph), range 13800 km (8,625 miles)

Dimensions: wing span 60.30 m (197 ft 10 in), length 59.39 m (194 ft 10 in), height 16.74 m (54 ft 11 in)

Recognition features
A Four-engined wide body
B Winglets
C High aspect-ratio wings

Agusta A 119 Koala   *Italy*

The A 119 Koala entered production in 1999 and is closely based on the A 109. It is powered by a single P&WC PT6B turboshaft and is an obvious replacement for aging JetRanger and Hughes 500 helicopters. By the beginning of 2000 in excess of 20 Koalas had been ordered.

Recognition features
A Skid landing gear
B Large single window in sliding cabin doors
C Dorsal and ventral tail fins

Agusta A 109   *Italy*

The A 109 is a highly flexible executive helicopter which has also fulfilled a variety of military roles. First flown on 4 August 1971 the twin-engined A 109 has capacity for seven passengers and a pilot and has been steadily improved to the most recent A 109E Power (right) standard. The aircraft is powered by either P&WC PW206 or Turboméca Arriel turboshafts, according to model and specification.

Recognition features
A Retractable tricycle U/C
B Sharply-pointed nose section
C Dorsal and ventral fins

Avia-Pitts S-2   *USA*

First flown in 1967, the Pitts S-2 was a stretched two-seat version of the popular S-1 Pitts Special aerobatic aircraft. Aerotek subsequently put the S-2 into production as the the S-2A, and later produced the S-2B and S-2S. Aviat introduced the S-2C (right) in 1998 with a squared-off vertical tail and other modifications.

Recognition features
A Small size
B Fixed tailwheel U/C
C Biplane configuration

18

Antonov An-124 Ruslan

Ukraine

Originally designed for a Russian military requirement, the An-124 is the largest commercial freighter generally available and is in demand due to its ability to carry very heavy outsize loads. First flown on 26 December 1982, it has an upward-opening nose section and tail ramp to allow through-loading of freight and palletised cargo. An upper deck is incorporated with seating for up to 88 passengers. Around 52 An-124s have been flown and the majority of these are in commercial service. The latest An-124 models include the An-124-100M (introduced in 2000) with Progress D-18T Series 3 turbofans and the abortive An-124-210 powered by Rolls-Royce RB.211s. Antonov is also considering the An-124-200 with GE CF6-80C2 engines and Aviastar has also proposed a similar version with a modernised cockpit which it designates An-124-130.

An-124-100M
Powerplant: four 229.50-kN (51,590-lb st) Lotarev D-18T turbofans

Performance: max speed 865 km/h (537 mph), cruising speed 800 km/h (497 mph), take-off run 2520 m (8,270 ft), range 16500 km (10,313 miles)

Dimensions: wing span 73.30 m
(240 ft 6 in), length 69.10 m (226
ft 8 in), height 20.78 m (68 ft 2 in)

Recognition features
A High-wing configuration
B Huge size
C Tall, broad-chord tail fin
D Five-bogie main U/C

Antonov An-140

Ukraine

The An-140 was developed as a replacement for the An-24 and An-26 on short-haul routes in the Eastern Bloc countries. Its design layout follows the familiar Antonov philosophy with a high wing and externally mounted U/C. Seating capacity is for 52 passengers in standard form and up to 80 in high density, and the An-140 is powered by a pair of turboprops mounted on the inboard wing section. Plans are in hand for further versions with Western engines, particularly the P&WC PW127A licence-built by Klimov. The first of two prototype An-140s made its first flight on 17 September 1997, although Ukrainian production was suspended on 7 June 2001. An agreement signed in late 1999 allows for the An-140 to be built under licence in Iran. The first Iranian-built An-140, the IRAN 140, flew on 7 February 2001.

An-140
Powerplant: two 1839-kW (2,466 shp) Klimov TV3-117VMA-SB2 turboprops

Performance: max speed (estimated) 593 km/h (368 mph), cruising speed (estimated) 565 km/h (351 mph), take-off run (1341 m (4,400 ft), range 2100 km (1,313 miles)

Dimensions: wing span 24.25 m
(79 ft 7 in), length 22.46 m (73 ft
8 in), height 8.04 m (26 ft 4 in)

Recognition features
A High-aspect ratio wings
B Dihedralled, fuselage-mounted
tailplanes
C Tall, swept fin with prominent
fillet

ATR (Avions de Transport Regional) was formed in July 1980 by Aérospatiale and Aeritalia to produce a new regional airliner. Targeting the 42/50-passenger market, the ATR42 was announced in 1981 and the first ATR42-200 was flown on 16 August 1984. The first ATR42-300 with a strengthened structure was delivered in December 1985. The improved ATR42-320 was subsequently upgraded to ATR42-510 (above) standard with 6-blade propellers and other improvements. A 4.50-m (14-ft 9-in) fuselage stretch increased passenger capacity from 50 to 74 in the ATR72, which also has longer wings and increased tail fin area. ATR72 variants include the ATR72-210 and ATR72-510, which differ in engines, equipment fit, and specification.

ATR42-510
Powerplant: two 1611-kW (2,160 shp) Pratt & Whitney Canada PW127E turboprops

Performance: max speed 561 km/h (350 mph), cruising speed 515 km/h (322 mph), take-off run 1097 m (3,600 ft), range 1600 km (1,000 miles)

Dimensions: wing span 24.57 m
(80 ft 7 in), length 22.67 m (74 ft
5 in), height 7.59 m (24 ft 11 in)

Recognition features
A High-wing
B T-tail
C Twin engines in underslung
nacelles

BAe (Handley Page) Jetstream *UK*

The H.P.137 Jetstream was a light turboprop business and commuter aircraft designed by Handley Page and first flown on 18 August 1967. Forty were completed with Turboméca Astazou XIVC engines before Handley Page ceased operations in 1969. The Jetstream was taken over by Scottish Aviation (later BAe) which built 26 Jetstream T.Mk 1s for the RAF. These were followed by the Jetstream 31 which first flew on 28 March 1980. It sold widely in a 19-seat, single-aisle configuration. Later versions included the Jetstream 32 (Super 31, illustrated above) with a modified wing, higher gross weight, longer range and increased power. The last of 384 Jetstreams was completed in 1994 and large numbers remain in service worldwide.

Jetstream 31
Powerplant: two 760-kW (1,020-shp) Honeywell TPE331-12UAR turboprops

Performance: max speed 489 km/h (304 mph), cruising speed 452 km/h (280 mph), initial climb rate 683 m (2,240 ft) per min, range 1280 km (800 miles)

Dimensions: wing span 15.85 m
(52 ft), length 14.37 m (47 ft 1 in),
height 5.38 m (17 ft 8 in)

Recognition features
A Low wing
B Twin turboprops in narrow
nacelles
C Down-sloping nose profile

BAe 146 and Avro RJ

The BAe 146, originally a Hawker Siddeley project, was relaunched by BAe in 1978 and the prototype flew on 3 September 1981. It is a short-haul airliner powered by four pylon-mounted Honeywell turbofans. The standard BAe 146-100 has 93 passenger seats and the 146-200, which has a longer fuselage, has 109 seats. The 146-300, which first flew on 1 May 1987, has a further fuselage stretch. All models were also offered as 'QT' freighters. Some 35 BAe 146-100s were built together with 115 BAe 146-200s and 69 BAe 146-300s. In 1990, the line was relaunched as the 85-seat Avro RJ70 (formerly -100), 100-seat RJ85 (-200), 112-seat RJ100 and 116-seat RJ115 (-300) and over 150 RJs have been sold. The upgraded RJX series, to be powered by Honeywell AS977 engines, was abandoned by BAE Systems on 27 November 2001.

RJ100
Powerplant: four 31.10-kN (7,000-lb st) Honeywell LF507 turbofans

Performance: max speed 763 km/h (474 mph), cruising speed 720 km/h (445 mph), range 2742 km (1,714 miles)

Dimensions: wing span 26.20 m (86 ft), length 30.99 m (101 ft 8 in), height 8.60 m (28 ft 3 in)

Recognition features
A High-wing
B T-tail
C Four turbofan engines

Beech (Raytheon) 1900

In the early 1980s, with the Model 99 commuter airliner becoming obsolete, Beech designed a new turboprop which would offer significant improvements. The Model 1900 was based on the pressurised Model 200 with a stretched 19-passenger fuselage, a revised tail and redesigned wing. It first flew on 3 September 1982 and was sold as the standard 1900 and as the 1900C with a port rear cargo door. The later 1900C-1 has a modified fuel system and a wet wing. The 1900C has been delivered to the USAF as the C-12J and to the air forces of Taiwan and Egypt. Some 250 1900Cs were built. The 1900D (above), which first flew on 1 March 1990, has a deeper fuselage giving a stand-up cabin, and winglets. The 1900D replaced the 1900C in production and first deliveries were made in November 1991.

Beech 1900D
Powerplant: two 954-kW (1,279 shp) Pratt & Whitney PT6A-67D turboprops

Performance: max speed 534 km/h (334 mph), cruising speed 512 km/h (320 mph), take-off field length 1140 m (3,740 ft), initial climb rate 800 m (2,625 ft) per minute, range 1272 km (795 miles)

Dimensions: wing span 17.60 m (57 ft 9 in), length 17.60 m (57 ft 9 in), height 4.54 m (14 ft 11 in)

Recognition features
A Swept T-tail with finlets
B Large strakes beneath rear fuselage (single, smaller strake on 1900C)
C Low wing with winglets
D 'Humpback' fuselage of 1900D

Ayres Thrush   *USA*

The Thrush agplane has its origins in the Snow S-1 of 1953. Production S-2As, Bs and Cs were followed by the Rockwell S-2R. Ayres built Thrushes from 1977, most with turboprops (TPE331 or PT6A) and some with two-seats. Turbo Thrushes include the S2R-T34 (right).

Recognition features

A Low wing
B Prominent cockpit enclosure
C Long nose with turboprop engine

BAe Jetstream 41   *UK*

BAe flew the prototype 29-seat Jetstream 41 on 25 September 1991. It was based on the J31 but with a 4.88-m (16 ft) fuselage stretch, a larger fin, EFIS cockpit and higher gross weight. The wing incorporated additional baggage capacity. New 1119-kW (1,500 shp) TPE331-14 turboprops were fitted. Some 104 J41s had been built when production ceased in 1998.

Recognition features

A Low wing
B Mid-set tailplane
C Similar to, but larger than, J31

Bell Model 206 JetRanger   *USA*

The Model 206 lost the 1960 US Army LOH competition, but became popular as a light civil helicopter. It was later built as the military Kiowa and Kiowa Warrior, and Sea Ranger. The five-seat JetRanger is powered by a Rolls-Royce 250-C turboshaft. It first flew on 10 January 1966 and variants include the 206L Long Ranger. The Model 407 has a four-bladed main rotor and a wider cabin.

Recognition features

A Twin-bladed main rotor (all 206s)
B Dorsal and ventral fins

Beriev Be-200 *Russia*

Beriev has designed a large commercial utility amphibian, the Be-200, which is aimed at a range of civilian applications. First flown on 24 September 1998, it follows the general layout of the earlier A-40 Albatross but has a much deeper and wider fuselage which can accommodate up to 66 passengers in a pressurised cabin, or nine freight containers. The Be-200 has a T-tail and twin D-436 turbofans mounted on rear fuselage pylons. It has fly-by-wire systems and a modern technology cockpit. A principal role will be aerial firefighting for which it is equipped with a scoop system and capacity for 12 tonnes of water in underfloor tanks and is designated Be-200ChS. The Be-200 will also be used for air-sea rescue, ambulance and military patrol duties and has been ordered by the Russian Emergency Action Ministry and the Forestry Ministry.

Powerplant: two 73.60-kN (16,550-lb st) ZMKB-Progress D-436TP turbofans

Performance: max speed 700 km/h (435 mph), cruising speed 550 km/h (341 mph), initial climb rate 840 m (2,755 ft) per min, range 2000 km (1,250 miles)

Dimensions: wing span 32.78 m (107 ft 6 in), length 29.18 m (95 ft 9 in), height 8.90 m (29 ft 2 in)

Recognition features
A Boat-like hull
B Retractable tricycle U/C
C Dorsally-mounted twin turbofan engines

Boeing 717/McDD MD-80/90 *USA*

On 18 October 1979, McDonnell Douglas flew the first DC-9-81 (MD-81, above) which was a major upgrade of the successful DC-9. The fuselage was stretched to give 172-passenger capacity and other changes included a modified fin with a bulged tip, modified flaps, increased fuel capacity and JT8D-209 turbofans. Further MD-80 variants included the shorter 139-seat MD-87 and 158-seat MD-90-30. Some 28 MD-82s were built in China by SAIC. The MD-90 series features 111.12-kN (25,000 lb st) IAE V2528-D5 turbofans. Following Boeing's take-over of McDonnell Douglas in 1997, the 100-seat MD-95 was relaunched as the Boeing 717-200 with the 80-seat Boeing 717-100 and 120-seat Boeing 717-300 not being built. The 717-200 differs from earlier variants primarily in having Rolls-Royce Deutschland BR715 turbofans.

MD-83
Powerplant: two 93.42-kN (21,000-lb st) Pratt & Whitney JT8D-219 turbofans

Performance: max speed 918 km/h (574 mph), cruising speed 880 km/h (550 mph), range 4608 km (2,880 miles)

Dimensions: wing span 32.87 m
(107 ft 10 in), length 45.07 m
(147 ft 10 in), height 9.04 m
(29 ft 8 in)

Recognition features
A Rear-mounted engines and
T-tail
B Long, narrow fuselage
C High-aspect ratio wings

Boeing 737

USA

The 124-seat 737-100 first flew on 9 April 1967. The stretched, 136-seat 737-200 (above) first flew on 8 August 1967, while the 737-300 of 1981, had a further fuselage stretch and was powered by CFM56 turbofans. The 737-400, flown on 29 April 1988, had an additional stretch raising capacity to 168 passengers. The -200 received a facelift in 1989 as the 108-seat 737-500 which used the same fuselage but had longer wings, the -300 tail and CFM56s. The 132-seat 737-600 'next-generation' development of the -500 first flew on 22 January 1998 with changes including an EFIS cockpit. Similarly, the -300 was upgraded as the 149-seat 737-700 and the -400 became the 189-seat 737-800. The further-stretched 737-900 was first delivered in May 2001. BBJ variants of the -700 and -800 are available.

737-300
Powerplant: two 88.97-kN (20,000-lb st) CFM International CFM56-3B1 turbofans

Performance: max speed 855 km/h (530 mph), cruising speed 816 km/h (510 mph), take-off run 2635 m (8,650 ft), range 4554 km (2,830 miles) at optional higher weight

38

Dimensions: wing span 28.88 m (94 ft 9 in), length 33.40 m (109 ft 7 in), height 11.13 m (36 ft 6 in)

Recognition features
A Low-wing
B Engines carried flush with wing on 737-100/200; otherwise on short pylons
C Flat-bottomed engine nacelles on all but 737-100/200

Boeing 747 *USA*

Boeing first flew its revolutionary 747-100 on 9 February 1969. The type was followed by the higher-weight 747-200, developments of which included Combi and Freighter versions, the later with an upward-hinging nose door; the short-fuselage, long-range 747SP; and the USAF's E-4. Demand for even more seats than the maximum 551 capacity of the standard 747-200B led to Boeing developing a longer upper deck for the 747-300. The first of these flew in 1982, the type later forming the basis of the 747-400 (above), which introduced winglets, a much revised and lighter structure, a new EFIS cockpit and extra tailplane fuel tanks. The first -400 flew in August 1988. As with earlier 747 models, customers have a choice of powerplants including the P&W PW4056, Rolls-Royce RB.211-524G and General Electric CF6-80C2B1F.

747-400
Powerplant: (typical) four 206.86-kN (46,500-lb st) Pratt & Whitney PW4056 turbofans

Performance: max speed 979 km/h (612 mph), cruising speed 944 km/h (590 mph), range 13416 km (8,385 miles)

Dimensions: wing span 64.44 m
(211 ft 5 in), length 70.70 m
(231 ft 10 in), height 19.40 m
(63 ft 8 in)

Recognition features
A Bulged fairing over forward
fuselage
B Four engines
C Huge size

Boeing 757 USA

The gap in range and passenger capacity between the 727 and the 747 was filled by the short/medium-range 757 and the medium/long-range 767. The Boeing 757-200 (above) first flew on 18 February 1982. It features six-abreast single-aisle seating for up to 239 passengers and a large underfloor freight hold. Engines may be P&W PW2037 or Rolls-Royce RB.211-535C turbofans. The first 757-200 delivery to British Airways took place in January 1983 and other early aircraft went to Eastern Airlines, Monarch Airlines and Delta. The 757-200CB is a combi version and the 757-200PF is a specialised small package freighter for United Parcel Service. The new 757-300 is a larger-capacity version with a 7.11-m (23-ft 4-in) fuselage stretch and the prototype flew on 2 August 1998. The RB.211-powered 757-300 first entered service with Condor Flugdienst.

757-200
Powerplant: (typical) two 169.90-kN (38,200-lb st) Rolls-Royce RB.211-535C turbofans

Performance: max speed 1046 km/h (654 mph), cruising speed 980 km/h (609 mph), take-off run 1676 m (5,500 ft), range 4728 km (2,955 miles)

Dimensions: wing span 38.05 m (124 ft 10 in), length 47.32 m (155 ft 3 in), height 13.56 m (44 ft 6 in)

Recognition features
A Low-wing
B Two large turbofans in underwing nacelles
C Forward fuselage has drooped appearance

43

Boeing 767

The medium/long-range Boeing 767 was developed alongside the 757 and while it follows a similar design layout it has a different wing and a wider fuselage with twin-aisle seven-abreast economy seating and 290-passenger maximum capacity. The prototype 767-200 first flew on 26 September 1981. Powerplants include the JT9D-7R4D, GE CF6-80C2 and Rolls-Royce RB.211-524G turbofans. The 767-300 (above) is a larger-capacity model with a 6.40-m (21-ft) fuselage stretch and up to 360 seats and both versions are also sold as extended-range models as the 767-200ER and 767-300ER respectively. The 767-400ER is a -300 with a further 6.45-m (21-ft 2-in) fuselage extension, an upgraded flight deck and longer wings with raked wingtips. It was first flown on 9 October 2000. Almost 900 Boeing 767s had been ordered by the end of 2000.

767-200
Powerplant: (typical) two 213.54-kN (48,000-lb st) Pratt & Whitney JT9D-7R4D turbofans

Performance: max speed 992 km/h (620 mph), cruising speed 960 km/h (600 mph), range 6984 km (4,365 miles)

Dimensions: wing span 47.57 m
(156 ft 1 in), length 48.50 m
(159 ft 2 in), height 15.85 m
(52 ft)

Recognition features
A Wide-body fuselage
B Blunt nose section ahead of
cockpit
C Clean wing

Boeing 777 *USA*

Outwardly resembling a scaled-up 767 with two large underwing turbofans, the 777 has a main cabin twin-aisle layout with nine/ten-abreast seating. In high-density configuration, the 777-200 seats 440 passengers. The prototype first flew on 12 June 1994 and Boeing also offers the 777-200ER version with additional centre-section tankage and higher payload. The choice of engines includes the GE90-76B, Rolls-Royce Trent 877 and P&W PW4077. Uprated versions of these are used on the stretched Boeing 777-300, the world's longest airliner, which first flew on 16 October 1997 and offers a maximum capacity of 550 seats. A 777-300ER version will be available in 2005. More than 500 777s had been ordered by the end of 2000.

777-200
Powerplant: (typical) two 350.08-kN (78,700-lb st) General Electric GE90-76B turbofans

Performance: max speed 1059 km/h (662 mph), cruising speed 1022 km/h (639 mph), take-off run 2530 m (8,300 ft), range 9480 km (5,925 miles)

Dimensions: wing span 60.93 m
(199 ft 11 in), length 63.73 m
(209 ft 1 in), height 18.52 m
(60 ft 9 in)

Recognition features
A Tall, narrow-chord fin
B Triple-wheel main U/C bogies
C Large-diameter engine nacelles

Bell 427   *USA*

Based on the Model 206L Long Ranger, the Model 407 has a four-blade main rotor and wider cabin, and formed the basis of the further revised six-passenger Model 427. With space for EMS equipment, the Model 427 first flew on 15 December 1997, and is powered by two 466-kW (625-shp) P&WC PW207D turboshafts.

Recognition features
A Skid landing gear
B Endplate fins on tailplanes
C Wide fuselage

BAe ATP/Jetstream 61   *UK*

With many Hawker Siddeley HS.748s in service, BAe developed a larger-capacity version. First flown on 6 August 1986 as the ATP, this involved a major redesign with a 5.01-m (16-ft 6-in) fuselage stretch for 64 passengers. P&W PW126s driving six-blade propellers power the ATP, which was renamed Jetstream 61 in 1996.

Recognition features
A Six-blade propellers
B Large fin fillet
C High-aspect ratio wings

Beriev Be-12 Chaika   *Russia*

The Be-12 Chaika (NATO codename 'Mail') is a large amphibian designed for military duties. It first flew in 1960. The military Be-12 normally flies with a crew of five and the watertight doors covering the aircraft's large internal weapons bay have made it an ideal choice for use in a firebombing role. It has been marketed as the Be-12M-300 for this and other commercial duties.

Recognition features
A Twin turboprops
B Deep boat hull
C Retractable tricycle U/C
D Gull wing

Bombardier Challenger

Canada

Originally conceived by Bill Lear as the Learstar 600, the Challenger first flew on 8 November 1978. Designated CL-600-1A11, it is an intercontinental business jet with a wide-body interior normally accommodating 14 executive passengers, and two rear fuselage-mounted turbofans. First deliveries were made in 1980 and several military and special missions variants have been sold. The Challenger 601 has CF34-1A engines and winglets and has been produced in variants including the long-range 601-3A-ER and 601-3R (above). The Challenger 604 is a development of the 601-3R with a new belly fairing, extra rear fuselage fuel tanks, a larger cabin and CF34-3B engines. More than 500 aircraft of the Challenger series have been delivered.

Challenger 604
Powerplant: two 41-kN (9,220-lb st) General Electric CF34-3B1 turbofans

Performance: max speed 880 km/h (548 mph), cruising speed 850 km/h (530 mph), initial climb rate 549 m (1,800 ft) per min, range 7500 km (4,690 miles)

Dimensions: wing span 19.60 m
(64 ft 4 in), length 20.85 m
(68 ft 5 in), height 6.30 m
(20 ft 8 in)

Recognition features
A T-tail
B Distinctive engine nacelle
shape
C Winglets from Challenger 601

Bombardier CL-215/CL-415 *Canada*

The CL-215 is the only modern large civil utility amphibian to have been produced in quantity in the West. It is a high-wing all-metal aircraft intended for firefighting and utility work. The slab-sided fuselage has a planing bottom with a large ventral hatch for dumping a 5346-litre (1,412- US gal) load of retardant. The CL-215, powered by two 1569-kW (2,100-hp) P&W CA-3 Double Wasp piston engines, first flew on 23 October 1967. The CL-215T (above) features PW123AFs, wingtip endplates and auxiliary fins on the tailplane. As the CL-415 production aircraft, fitted with an EFIS cockpit, this replaced the CL-215 in production. The CL-415M is a special missions version.

CL-415
Powerplant: two 1775-kW (2,380-shp) Pratt & Whitney PW123AF turboprops

Performance: max speed 362 km/h (227 mph), cruising speed 331 km/h (207 mph), initial climb rate 419 m (1,375 ft) per min, range 2410 km (1,506 miles)

Dimensions: wing span 28.60 m
(93 ft 11 in), length 19.82 m
(65 ft), height 8.98 m (29 ft 6 in)

Recognition features
A High wing
B Boat hull
C Retractable tricycle U/C
D Large wing endplates on
CL-215T and CL-415

Bombardier CRJ

Canada

The Challenger was the basis for development of the Canadair Regional Jet (CRJ) regional airliner and the Global Express long-range business jet. The CRJ is based on the Challenger 601-3A with a 6.10 m (20 ft) longer fuselage and accommodation for up to 50 passengers. The prototype first flew on 10 May 1991 and the first delivery was made in October 1992. Some have also been built as the Corporate Jetliner (above) for high-density executive use. Almost 1,000 CRJs have been ordered, many of them CRJ100s with CF34-3A1 engines. The CRJ200 has improved engines with lower fuel consumption, while the CRJ700 which first flew on 27 May 1999, has a stretched fuselage to accommodate 70 passengers and a deeper and wider cabin. It is available in standard or extended-range versions. The further-stretched CRJ900 flew for the first time on 21 February 2001.

CRJ200
Powerplant: two 41-kN (9,220-lb st) General Electric CF34-3B1 turbofans

Performance: max speed 859 km/h (534 mph), cruising speed 786 km/h (488 mph), initial climb rate 1128 m (3,700 ft) per min, range 1777 km (1,110 miles)

Dimensions: wing span 21.21 m (69 ft 7 in), length 26.77 m (87 ft 10 in), height 6.22 m (20 ft 5 in)

Recognition features
A T-tail
B All versions have winglets
C Short U/C legs give low sit on ground

Bombardier DHC-8 Dash 8 *Canada*

De Havilland Canada designed the DHC-8 Dash 8 as a turboprop commuter design which could be developed into a family of local service airliners. The first 40-passenger DHC-8-100 (above) first flew on 20 June 1983. It was immediately successful with Canadian regional operators and feeder airlines serving American trunk operators. The DHC-8-200 has a higher gross weight and 1603-kW (2,150-shp) PW123C engines and the DHC-8-300, which first flew on 15 May 1987, has a 56-passenger stretched fuselage and increased power. The DHC-8-400 is a further stretched variant first flown on 31 January 1998, with a maximum 78-seat capacity. The Dash 8 variants are now built by Bombardier in Dash 8 Q100, Q200, Q300 and Q400 configuration with an active noise suppression system.

DHC-8-300A
Powerplant: two 1775-kW (2,380-shp) Pratt & Whitney Canada PW123 turboprops

Performance: max speed 528 km/h (330 mph), cruising speed 480 km/h (300 mph), initial climb rate 549 m (1,800 ft) per min, range 1520 km (950 miles)

Dimensions: wing span 27.43 m (90 ft), length 25.68 m (84 ft 3 in), height 7.49 m (24 ft 7 in)

Recognition features
A High wing
B T-tail
C Underslung engines
D Main U/C retracts into engine nacelles

Bombardier Global Express *Canada*

The Bombardier BD700 Global Express intercontinental business jet is externally similar to the Challenger but is 50% larger and is, essentially, a new design with a new wing and stretched fuselage. It has a wide-body cabin for between eight and 19 executive passengers and was first flown on 13 October 1996, powered by two BMW Rolls-Royce (now Rolls-Royce Deutschland) BR710 turbofans. The Global Express is aimed at business users requiring non-stop very-long-range capability at a high cruise speed over routes such as New York to Tokyo, or Sydney to Los Angeles. It is also designed for good short-field performance. The first aircraft entered service in July 1999 and in excess of 120 firm orders had been received by October 2001. The shortened, eight-passenger Global 5000 is due to make its first flight in 2003.

Powerplant: two 65.30-kN (14,690-lb st) Rolls-Royce Deutschland BR710A2-20 turbofans

Performance: max speed 950 km/h (590 mph), cruising speed 850 km/h (530 mph), initial climb rate 1097 m (3,600 ft) per min, range 12336 km (7,710 miles)

Dimensions: wing span 28.65 m
(94 ft), length 30.30 m
(99 ft 5 in), height 7.57 m
(24 ft 10 in)

Recognition features
A T-tail
B Winglets
C Square cabin windows
D Large wingroot fairing

Britten Norman BN-2 Islander *UK*

The Islander light twin was designed by John Britten and Desmond Norman as a simple multi-purpose utility aircraft with a ten-seat cabin. The BN-2 prototype first flew on 20 August 1966 powered by 194-kW (260-hp) Lycoming O-540-E4B5 engines. Over 1,175 have been built, variants including the BN-2A-2 and BN-2B (above). The Defender is a military model and turbine variants include the BN-2A-41 Turbo Islander, which first flew on 6 April 1977, with Lycoming LTP-101 turboprops and the BN-2T with 239-kW (320-shp) Allison 250-B17Cs. Britten Norman has marketed the CASTOR BN-2T with a large nose radome for maritime surveillance and now builds the BN-2T-4 Defender 4000 with a larger wing, stretched fuselage and 298-kW (400-shp) 250-B17F turboprops.

BN-2B Islander
Powerplant: two 194-kW (260-hp) Textron Lycoming O-540-E4C5 piston engines

Performance: max speed 274 km/h (170 mph), cruising speed 258 km/h (160 mph), initial climb rate 262 m (860 ft) per min, range 1175 km (735 miles)

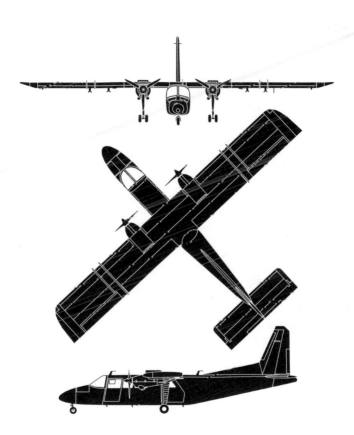

Dimensions: wing span 14.94 m
(49 ft), length 10.86 m
(35 ft 8 in), height 4.18 m
(13 ft 9 in)

Recognition features
A Fixed tricycle U/C
B Square-section cabin
C High-mounted 'plank' wing
D Noisy piston engines

Cessna 172 Skyhawk family   *USA*

The Model 172 Skyhawk is the most popular four-seat lightplane ever, with over 43,000 examples of the range completed by mid-1999. The 172 (right) first flew on 12 June 1955 with a straight, squared-off fin. Variants feature swept fins, a rear-view 'omnivision' cabin window and various Lycoming and Continental engines. The high-power Model 175, military T-41, Reims-built FR172 Reims Rocket and retractable U/C Model 172RG have also been built.

Recognition features
A Most models have fixed tricycle U/C
B High wing

Cessna 500/501 Citation & 525 CitationJet   *USA*

The eight-seat Citation 500 bizjet first flew on 15 September 1969. The later Citation I was followed by the Model 501 Citation I/SP. In 1985 the Model 550 entered production, while the Model 525 CitationJet first flew on 29 April 1991 as an entry-level bizjet. It is available as the CJ-1 or CJ-2 (right).

Recognition features
A Long, rounded nose
B Low, dihedralled, wing

Commander 112 and 114   *USA*

Rockwell International designed the Model 111, 112 and 114 with a four-seat airframe and different engine and U/C configurations. Production versions included the Commander 112, 112TC, 114, 114A (Grand Turismo) and 429. The 114B and 114TC (right) were introduced in 1992 by Commander Aircraft. The 115 and 115TC have a modified wing.

Recognition features
A Retractable U/C
B Low wing

Cessna 550, 551, 552 and 560 Citation *USA*

The Model 550 Citation II was a stretched, 12-seat development of the Model 500 with uprated JT15D-4 engines. The Model 551 Citation II/SP was an alternative version certificated for single-pilot operation. Cessna also built the improved S550 Citation S/II with a modified wing section for a gross weight increase and this was sold to the US Navy as the T-47A trainer. The current model is the 550 Citation Bravo with a seven-passenger cabin. In 1987, the Model 560 Citation V was introduced with a further stretched fuselage. This has been upgraded to become the Citation Ultra Encore with increased load and performance, improved avionics and EFIS. Many Citation IIs and Vs have found military applications, including the Spanish Air Force TR.20 (above) which is fitted with a SLAR pod.

Citation V Ultra Encore
Powerplant: two 14.95-kN (3,360-lb st) Pratt & Whitney PW535A turbofans

Performance: max speed 796 km/h (495 mph), cruising speed 768 km/h (480 mph), initial climb rate 1289 m (4,230 ft) per min, range 3610 km (2,255 miles)

Dimensions: wing span 15.91 m
(52 ft 2 in), length 14.90 m
(48 ft 10 in), height 4.57 m (15 ft)

Recognition features
A Compound sweep on wing
leading edge
B Mid-set, dihedralled tailplane
C Rounded nose

Cessna 560XL Citation Excel

USA

The Citation Excel business jet was introduced to provide an aircraft to fit between the Citation Ultra and the Citation VII with performance equivalent to the Ultra. The Excel uses a shorter version of the Citation X fuselage which gives capacity for seven passengers in a full stand-up cabin. This is combined with the wing of the Citation 560 Ultra and higher-thrust PW545A turbofans mounted on the rear fuselage. The prototype Excel first flew on 29 February 1996 and it is in current production with over 175 delivered by the end of 2000.

Powerplant: two 16.92-kN (3,804-lb st) Pratt & Whitney PW545A turbofans

Performance: max speed 791 km/h (494 mph), cruising speed 754 km/h (471 mph), initial climb rate 940 m (3,090 ft) per min, range 3827 km (2,392 miles)

Dimensions: wing span 16.98 m
(55 ft 8 in), length 15.79 m
(51 ft 9 in), height 5.24 m
(17 ft 2 in)

Recognition features
A Dihedralled tailplane
B Short U/C legs
C Fuselage shape similar to
Citation X

Cessna 750 Citation X

Cessna's flagship business jet, the Citation X, made its first flight on 21 December 1993. It was designed to give long-range, high-speed performance with smaller capacity than the Gulfstream IV but equivalent comfort for passengers. It cruises at Mach 0.92 and at altitudes of up to 15545 m (51,000 ft). The Cessna 750 is a completely new design, featuring a swept wing and prominent T-tail. As with the earlier Model 650 Citation VII, the wing is set below the fuselage line and the internal cabin height of 1.75 m (5 ft 8 in) allows passengers to walk around without stooping. The Citation X is normally fitted with eight main cabin seats together with a galley and lavatory. Citation X deliveries reached 142 at the end of December 2000.

Powerplant: two 28.47-kN (6,400-lb st) Rolls-Royce AE3007C turbofans

Performance: max speed 1120 km/h (700 mph), cruising speed 1094 km/h (684 mph), initial climb rate 1341 m (4,400 ft) per min, range 6072 km (3,795 miles)

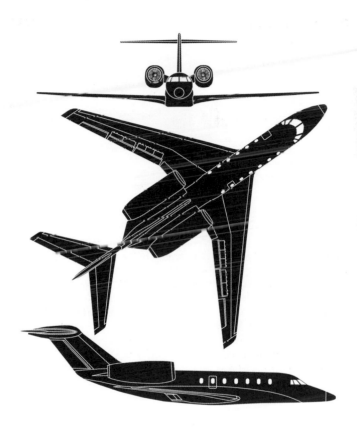

Dimensions: wing span 19.48 m
(63 ft 11 in), length 22 m
(72 ft 2 in), height 5.77 m
(18 ft 11 in)

Recognition features
A Sharply swept, high-aspect
ratio wing
B Large engine nacelles
C Large wing root fairing

Cirrus Design SR.20 *USA*

Cirrus Design is one of the first US companies to have applied composite technology to a high-volume production light aircraft. Its SR.20 four-seater is intended as the first in a family of aircraft which will include versions with larger cabins and retractable gear. It has a modern cockpit with a central navigation display and side sticks instead of the more conventional control columns. The most radical feature is a Ballistic Recovery System consisting of an emergency parachute housed behind the cockpit which can be activated to save the aircraft in the case of a power failure. The SR.20 prototype made its first flight on 31 March 1995 and went into series production in 1999 with 644 on order by late 2000. The SR.22 is a higher powered version with a 231-kW (310-hp) IO-550N engine.

SR.20
Powerplant: one 149-kW (200-hp) Teledyne Continental IO-360-ES piston engine

Performance: max speed 370 km/h (230 mph), cruising speed 296 km/h (185 mph), initial climb rate 275 m (900 ft) per min, range 1472 km (920 miles)

Dimensions: wing span 10.85 m
(35 ft 7 in), length 8 m
(26 ft 3 in), height 2.82 m
(9 ft 3 in)

Recognition features
A Fixed tricycle U/C
B Forward-raked nose U/C
C Low wing
D Bulged cabin roof line

Dassault Falcon 2000 *France*

The Falcon 2000 was designed to offer a similar range and speed performance to that of the Falcon 50 with a wider passenger cabin, similar to that of the Falcon 900. Operating economics are also improved by using two TFE738 turbofan engines, rather than the three TFE731s of the Falcon 50, to provide equivalent thrust. The passenger cabin is two-thirds the length of that of the Falcon 900, and can accommodate eight passengers in normal configuration. The cockpit is equipped with Dassault's new-generation EFIS and HUD equipment. The wing design is based on that of the Falcon 50 and Falcon 900 as is the tail unit. Dassault flew the first Falcon 2000 on 4 March 1993 and delivered the first customer aircraft in 1995. On 25 October 2001 the prototype Falcon 2000EX, offering 25% greater range, was flown for the first time.

Falcon 2000
Powerplant: two 26.33-kN (5,918-lb st) Honeywell TFE738-1-1B turbofans

Performance: max speed 885 km/h (553 mph), cruising speed 791 km/h (494 mph), initial climb rate 1658 m (5,440 ft) per min, range 5741 km (3,588 miles)

Dimensions: wing span 19.33 m
(63 ft 5 in), length 20.22 m
(66 ft 4 in), height 7.06 m
(23 ft 2 in)

Recognition features
A Anhedralled, mid-set tailplane
B Sharply-pointed nose
C Wide fuselage
D Clean swept wing

Dassault Falcon 900 *France*

Dassault's entrant in the large intercontinental business jet market is the Falcon 900. Following the Falcon 50's three-engined layout, the Falcon 900 has a similar wing design but a larger wide-body fuselage with a normal 12-passenger interior or high-density 19-seat cabin. The Falcon 900 prototype first flew on 21 September 1984, followed by first deliveries in 1986. The range of the 900 is 30% greater than that of the Falcon 50 and higher-thrust TFE731-5AR turbofans are used. The Falcon 900B, introduced in 1991, has TFE731-5BR engines for greater speed and range. The Falcon 900EX is a long-range model based on the 900B, which is also upgraded with a Honeywell Primus EFIS cockpit and headup display. The Falcon 900C is the latest variant with the avionics suite of the 900EX. A total of 260 Falcon 900s had been delivered by summer 2000.

Falcon 900EX
Powerplant: three 22.24-kN (5,000-lb st) Honeywell TFE731-60 turbofans

Performance: max speed 885 km/h (553 mph), cruising speed 791 km/h (494 mph), initial climb rate 1535 m (5,040 ft) per min, range 8280 km (5,175 miles)

Dimensions: wing span 19.33 m
(63 ft 5 in), length 20.21 m
(66 ft 4 in), height 7.55 m
(24 ft 9 in)

Recognition features
A Anhedralled mid-set tailplane
B Rear-mounted, triple-engine
layout
C Sharply-pointed nose

Dassault Falcon 50 *France*

Having achieved success with the short/medium-range Falcon 20 bizjet, Dassault designed the transcontinental Falcon 50 (right), which first flew on 7 November 1976. It uses the basic forward fuselage of the Falcon 20 married to a new wing and a rear fuselage mounting three TFE731-3 turbofans. The latest Falcon 50EX has an EFIS cockpit and more-powerful TFE731-40 engines.

Recognition features
A Compound sweep on wing
B Anhedralled tailplanes
C Triple-engine layout

Eagle XTS *Australia/Malaysia*

The Eagle XTS is an all-composite light aircraft. A single-seat proof-of-concept aircraft was built initially and the prototype side-by-side two-seat version first flew in 1988 powered by a 56-kW (75-hp) Aeropower engine. The production aircraft has dual controls and is available as the Eagle 150A or Eagle 150B, both with IO-240 engines, and some 25 had been sold by mid 2000.

Recognition features
A Two staggered wing surfaces
B Conventional tail
C Fixed tricycle U/C

EMBRAER EMB-110 Bandeirante *Brazil*

The Bandeirante airliner has its origins in the ten-passenger IPD-6504 project which flew as a prototype on 22 October 1968. EMBRAER was formed to build the production EMB-110. The type has PT6 turboprops and retractable tricycle U/C. Variants include the stretched EMB-110P1. Production ended in 1991.

Recognition features
A Twin turboprop
B Low wing
C Long fin fillet
D Narrow chord tailplane and fin

EMBRAER ERJ-135/145

Brazil

The EMB-145 (later ERJ-145) was based on the fuselage of the EMB-120 Brasilia turboprop, stretched and married to a modified tail unit and a new supercritical wing. The prototype first flew on 11 August 1995 and the type has seats for 50 passengers. The basic version became the ERJ-145ER (extended range), while the ERJ-145LR (long range) is also available. The ERJ-135 (above) is a 37-seat version with a shortened fuselage, and is also sold as the ECJ-135 Legacy bizjet. The prototype ERJ-135, converted from the ERJ-145 prototype, first flew on 4 July 1998. Embraer has also launched the EMB-145 AEW&C version and the EMB-145RS remote-sensing variant. The ERJ-145XR (extra long range) has higher weights, AE3007A1E engines, winglets and more fuel.

ERJ-145
Powerplant: two 31.32-kN (7,040-lb st) Rolls-Royce AE3007A turbofans

Performance: max speed 832 km/h (520 mph), cruising speed 792 km/h (495 mph), initial climb rate 777 m (2,550 ft) per min, range 2632 km (1,645 miles)

Dimensions: wing span 20.04 m
(65 ft 9 in), length 29.87 m
(98 ft), height 6.75 m (22 ft 2 in)

Recognition features
A T-tail
B Rear-mounted engines
C Only -145XR has winglets
D Longer U/C than CRJ

Fairchild Dornier 328JET

Germany/USA

Fairchild Aerospace found that the Do 328 would make an ideal platform for development of a regional jet to compete with aircraft such as the ERJ-135. The prototype 328JET was converted from an existing 328 airframe with the turboprop engines removed and two PW306/9 turbofans fitted in underwing pylon-mounted pods. A pair of ventral fins was also fitted on the rear fuselage and the aircraft has a strengthened wing, some aerodynamic wing modifications and larger flaps. It first flew on 20 January 1998 and has been certificated as a derivative of the 328. It is being sold with a 34-seat commuter cabin or as a bizjet named Envoy 3. A stretched version, the 428JET, was proposed with a longer fuselage, larger wing and PW308 engines.

Powerplant: two 26.90-kN (6,050-lb st) Pratt & Whitney PW306/9 turbofans

Performance: max speed 740 km/h (460 mph), cruising speed 712 km/h (445 mph), initial climb rate 686 m (2,250 ft) per min, range 1656 km (1,035 miles)

Dimensions: wing span 20.98 m
(68 ft 10 in), length 21.28 m
(69 ft 10 in), height 7.24 m
(23 ft 9 in)

Recognition features
A T-tail
B Straight, high-set wing
C Large pylon-mounted
underwing engine nacelles
D 'Humpback' shape

Fokker F28 Fellowship, F70/100   *Netherlands*

Fokker flew the prototype F28 on 9 May 1967. It was a 65-passenger regional airliner which provided a step-up for airlines using the F27 Friendship. The F28-1000 had 43.36-kN (9,750 lb st) Rolls-Royce Spey Mk 555-15 turbofans and it entered service in 1969. The stretched F28-2000 had a 79-passenger capacity and the F28-4000 was an upgrade of this model with a longer-span wing and 44.03-kN (9,900 lb st) Spey Mk 555-15H engines. Fokker also built a few F28-3000s with the -1000 fuselage and the engines and other improvements of the -4000 and two F28-6000s with full-span leading edge slats. The F28 was followed by the Fokker 100 (above) which has a further fuselage stretch for 122-passenger capacity, a longer wing, upgraded flight deck and Tay engines. The 80-seat F70 has a shorter fuselage and production of both types ceased when Fokker was declared insolvent in 1996.

F100
Powerplant: two 61.60-kN (13,850-lb st) Rolls-Royce Tay Mk 620-15 turbofans

Performance: max speed 853 km/h (530 mph), cruising speed 805 km/h (500 mph), initial climb rate 1855 m (6,085 ft) per min, range 2376 km (1,485 miles)

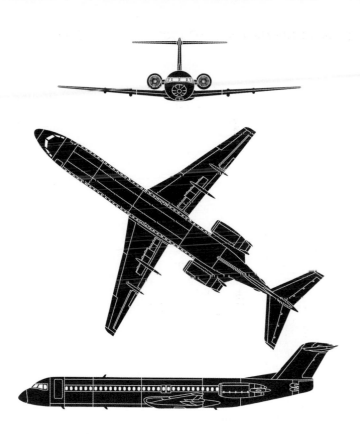

Dimensions: wing span 28.07 m
(92 ft 1 in), length 35.53 m
(116 ft 7 in), height 8.48 m
(27 ft 10 in)

Recognition features
A T-tail
B Low wing with prominent flap
track fairings
C Rear-mounted engines

Eurocopter Dauphin & EC 155   *France*

The eight/ten-passenger Dauphin helicopter was designed by Sud Aviation. The initial SA 360 first flew on 2 June 1972 with fixed tailwheel undercarriage and a single engine. The SA 365 Dauphin 2 has twin-engines and the SA 365N is a stretched version. The new EC 155 (AS 365N4) (right) has a wider fuselage and five-blade rotor.

Recognition features
A Fenestron tail rotor
B Most with retractable tricycle U/C

Eurocopter EC 120 B Colibri   *International*

Eurocopter inherited the EC 120 Colibri light business helicopter which had been initiated by Aérospatiale in 1990. This high-performance helicopter has five seats and a large rear baggage hold. The prototype was first flown on 9 June 1995. The production standard EC 120 B has a 376-kW (504-shp) Turboméca Arrius 2F turboshaft engine and is built by an international consortium including Eurocopter, ST Aero and CATIC.

Recognition features
A Fenestron tail rotor
B Tall skid U/C
C Three-blade main rotor

Eurocopter EC 135   *France/Germany*

The EC 135 is a larger companion to the EC 120 for seven passengers. Its design originated with the Bo 108 created by MBB. The EC 135 first flew on 15 February 1994 and can take stretchers or long items of cargo. Power is provided by either two P&WC PWC206B (EC 135P) or Arrius 2B turboshafts (EC 135T, right).

Recognition features
A Fenestron tail rotor
B Sharply upswept rear fuselage with door

Galaxy Astra

Israel/USA

The Astra (above) is based on the IAI 1124 Westwind. However, it is virtually a new aircraft and offers a substantial improvement in operating economies and high-speed/long-range performance. The fuselage is deeper and the Astra has a high-technology swept wing which is mounted beneath the fuselage to give improved cabin volume. The Astra SP offers greater range and speed, and a new autopilot and EFIS. The Model 1125 Astra SPX is the current model with further improved performance, uprated powerplant, a new interior and small winglets. The Astra entered production in 1985 and 132 had been built by summer 2000, including two C-38As for the US ANG. The Astra SPX is now marketed by Galaxy Aerospace.

Model 1125 Astra SPX
Powerplant: two 18.90-kN (4,250-lb st) Honeywell TFE731-40R-200G turbofans

Performance: max cruising speed 867 km/h (539 mph), initial climb rate 1128 m (3,700 ft) per min, range 5987 km (3,742 miles)

Dimensions: wing span 16.64 m
(54 ft 7 in), length 16.96 m
(55 ft 7 in), height 5.54 m
(18 ft 2 in)

Recognition features
A Mid-set, swept dihedralled tailplane
B Rear-mounted twin engines
C Long nose

Galaxy Galaxy

Israel/USA

The Galaxy super-midsize bizjet was designed by IAI and is built in Israel and marketed in North America by Galaxy Aerospace. Externally, it follows similar lines to the IAI 1125 Astra with a cruciform tail unit and a forward airstair entry door for passengers and crew. It uses a developed version of the Astra's advanced-technology wing but it is a larger aircraft and seats eight passengers for long-range executive use or can also be used as a corporate shuttle with up to 18 seats. The Galaxy has full transatlantic range and is fitted with an advanced cockpit and systems. The prototype first flew on 25 December 1997, being certificated a year later, and first customer deliveries were made in 1999. Galaxy, formed by IAI and the Hyatt Corporation, was purchased by General Dynamics on 5 June 2001. The Astra and Galaxy are still built by IAI and finished and marketed by Galaxy Aerospace, however.

Powerplant: two 25.36-kN (5,700-lb st) Pratt & Whitney Canada PW306A turbofans

Performance: max speed 870 km/h (540 mph), cruising speed 820 km/h (510 mph), range 6672 km (4,170 miles)

Dimensions: wing span 17.73 m
(58 ft 2 in), length 18.97 m
(62 ft 3 in), height 6.53 m
(21 ft 5 in)

Recognition features
A Deep fuselage
B Swept, high-aspect ratio wing
C Air intake at base of fin

Gulfstream V

Externally similar to the Gulfstream IV, the GV (above) features full intercontinental range. It has a stretched fuselage which allows a standard cabin layout for up to 19 passengers, optional sleeping compartments and a full galley and restroom. The cockpit has been enlarged and upgraded and is provided with a crew rest area. The wing is based on that of the GIV but with greater area and improved aerodynamic efficiency, and the vertical tail is taller with a pronounced tip fairing. The first GV was flown on 28 November 1995 and more than 170 had been ordered by late 2000. The C-37A is a VIP version for the USAF. The improved GV-SP flew for the first time on 31 August 2001.

GV
Powerplant: two 65.60-kN (14,750-lb st) Rolls-Royce Deutschland BR710-48 turbofans

Performance: max speed 1065 km/h (662 mph), cruising speed 980 km/h (609 mph), initial climb rate 1277 m (4,188 ft) per min, range 11976 km (7,485 miles)

Dimensions: wing span 28.50 m
(93 ft 6 in), length 29.39 m
(96 ft 5 in), height 7.87 m
(25 ft 10 in)

Recognition features
A T-tail
B Large, rear-mounted engine
nacelles
C Oval cabin windows
D Fin tip fairing

Fokker F27 Friendship and 50   *Netherlands*

The 40-seat F27-100 was first flown on 24 November 1955. Later variants included the F27-200, F27-300 Combiplane and F27-400. Fairchild licence-built the F-27 and developed the stretched FH-227. Fokker built the stretched F27-500. This spawned the F50-100 (right) which first flew on 28 December 1985 with square cabin windows, an upgraded cockpit and P&W PW125B engines. The F50-300 is a hot-and-high variant.

Recognition features
A High wing
B Slender engine nacelles housing main U/C
C Six-blade propellers on F50

Kaman K-1200 K-Max   *USA*

The K-1200 K-Max was designed for external vertical lift applications. It is a large single-seat helicopter fitted with Kaman's intermeshing twin-rotor system. It has a fixed tricycle undercarriage which can be fitted with skis and has a large vertical fin and secondary fins on a small tailplane. It is powered by a T53 turboshaft. The prototype K-Max first flew on 23 December 1991.

Recognition features
A Unique configuration

Lancair IV   *USA*

Following the kit-built Lancair 320, Lance Neibauer designed the Lancair IV (right). Announced in June 1990, this has a carbon-fibre composite fuselage and is powered by a Continental TSIO-550 engine. The pressurised Lancair IVP is also built.

Recognition features
A Stalky, retractable tricycle U/C
B Swept fin

Ibis Ae 270   *Czech Republic/Taiwan*

Ibis Aerospace, which is a joint venture between Aero Vodochody in the Czech Republic and AIDC in Taiwan, has designed the Ae 270 multi-purpose aircraft and flew the first of three flying prototypes, an Ae 270 P on 25 July 2000. Of conventional all-metal construction, the Ae 270 is intended for various civil and military roles including 10-seat passenger transport, cargo carrying for which it has a large port-side loading door, air ambulance, maritime patrol and photo mapping. Two initial versions are proposed - the Ae 270 P (above) with a pressurised cabin, retractable tricycle U/C and PT6A-42A engine and the unpressurised Ae 270 W with a fixed U/C and a 579-kW (777-shp) Walter M601F turboprop, but the fifth prototype will have a higher powered PT6-66A engine.

Ae 270 P
Powerplant: one 634-kW (850-shp) Pratt & Whitney Canada PT6A-42A turboprop

Performance: max speed 408 km/h (254 mph), cruising speed 390 km/h (242 mph), range 2916 km (1,823 miles)

Dimensions: wing span 13.82 m
(45 ft 4 in), length 12.23 m
(40 ft 1 in), height 4.78 m
(15 ft 8 in)

Recognition features
A Low-wing
B Single turboprop
C Low-set tailplane

Ilyushin Il-103

Russia

The Il-103 was designed as a competitor for US-built four-seat touring aircraft. It is of all-metal construction and has an IO-360 engine, but later versions are expected to be offered with a 134-kW (180-hp) powerplant, and a higher-powered version with a retractable undercarriage is also proposed. The prototype Il-103 was first flown on 17 May 1994 and approximately 30 had been completed by mid 1999, with an order in hand for five for the Peruvian air force. The Il-103 is manufactured by the Lukhovitze factory of MiG-MAPO.

Powerplant: one 157-kW (210-hp) Teledyne Continental IO-360-ES piston engine

Performance: max speed 250 km/h (155 mph), cruising speed 225 km/h (140 mph), initial climb rate 300 m (984 ft) per min, range 1064 km (665 miles)

Dimensions: wing span 10.57 m
(34 ft 8 in), length 8 m
(26 ft 3 in), height 3.12 m
(10 ft 3 in)

Recognition features
A Low wing
B Fixed tricycle U/C
C Expansive cabin glazing
D Gull-wing doors

Ilyushin Il-114 *Russia*

The Ilyushin Il-114 is a 64-seat twin-turboprop aircraft of very similar appearance to the BAe ATP with a low wing and retractable tricycle undercarriage. It first flew on 29 March 1990 powered by Klimov TV7 engines driving six-blade composite propellers and is intended as a replacement for many of the large fleet of An-24s remaining in service. First deliveries were made to Uzbekistan Airways in July 1998. Ilyushin has also designed and flown a cargo version as the Il-114T. Also under development is the Il-114-100 (above) with 2051-kW (2,750-shp) P&WC PW127H engines for US and European airline customers. Approximately 12 prototypes and production aircraft had been completed by mid-1999 although few sales had been achieved.

Il-114
Powerplant: two 1864-kW (2,500-shp) Klimov TV7-117-3 turboprops

Performance: max speed 507 km/h (315 mph), cruising speed 483 km/h (300 mph), take-off run 1554 m (5,100 ft), range 4768 km (2,980 miles)

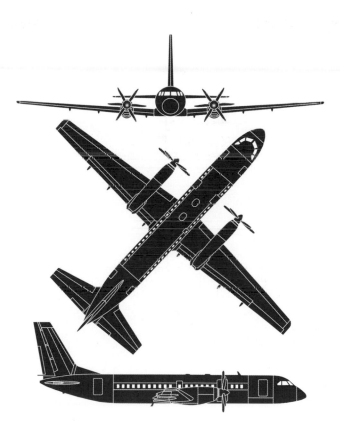

Dimensions: wing span 30 m
(98 ft 5 in), length 26.19 m
(85 ft 11 in), height 9.32 m
(30 ft 7 in)

Recognition features
A Blunt nose
B No cockpit 'eyebrow' windows

Ilyushin Il-96　　　　　　　　　　　　*Russia*

Problems with engine reliability and fuel economy resulted in a major redesign of the earlier Il-86. The Il-96 was, in many respects, a completely new aircraft with a new supercritical wing with winglets and redesigned flaps and leading edge slats. In initial form it was fitted with four Aviadvigatel PS-90A turbofans. The Il-86's lower-deck passenger boarding system was abandoned and the aircraft has fly-by-wire control systems and a modified tail and undercarriage. The prototype Il-96 flew on 28 September 1988 and is offered in standard (Il-96-300) form or as the stretched Il-96M with Pratt & Whitney PW2337 turbofans. The first Il-96-300s started to be delivered in 1992 to Aeroflot Russian International Airlines and Domodedovo Airlines and approximately 17 had been built by mid-2000. The Il-96T freighter (above) with a large forward port-side cargo door is also produced.

Il-96-300
Powerplant: four 156.92-kN (35,274-lb st) Aviadvigital PS-90A turbofans

Performance: max speed 901 km/h (560 mph), cruising speed 850 km/h (530 mph), range 13920 km (8,700 miles)

Dimensions: wing span 60.09 m
(197 ft 2 in), length 55.34 m
(181 ft 7 in), height 17.58 m
(57 ft 8 in)

Recognition features
A Four engines
B Winglets and broad-chord fin
D Triple-wheel main U/C

Liberty XL-2   *UK*

The Europa light aircraft is a high-performance two-seat kitplane. It is of composite construction and first flew in September 1992. Its side-by-side cockpit is fitted with dual controls and the latest Europa XS (monowheel right, foreground; tri-gear right, background) is powered by a choice of Rotax piston engines. High-aspect-ratio wings can be fitted to form a motor glider. The Liberty XL-2 is a mass-produced version launched in 2000.

Recognition features
A Retractable monowheel or fixed tricycle U/C
B Low cockpit profile

Maule M-5, M-6 & M-7   *USA*

In 1975, having built over 400 M-4s, Maule redesigned the type with a larger fin and other improvements. The basic model was the M-5-180C but a range of more powerful variants followed. The M-6-235 (right) was further improved. The current-production M-7 has a larger cabin and various U/C options. Variants include the turboprop M-7-420.

Recognition features
A Broad-chord, swept fin
B Twin-strut braced high wing

MBB (Eurocopter/Kawasaki) BK-117

In 1977, MBB and KHI started development of the 11-seat BK 117. A larger version of the Bo 105, it first flew on 13 June 1979. Variants include the twin LTS101-650-B-1-powered BK 117A-1, BK 117A-3, BK 117A-4, BK 117B-2 and BK 117C-1 with Arriel 1E engines.

Recognition features
A Clamshell rear loading doors
B Large endplate fins on tailplanes

Learjet 45

While the Learjet 45 is externally similar to the earlier Learjet series it is a completely new model which fits between the entry-level Model 31A and the larger Model 60. It has a redesigned wing with winglets, a deeper, nine-place, cabin than that of the Model 31A and substantially improved payload/range performance and handling characteristics. The Model 45 is equipped with an integrated avionics and flight instrumentation system. The prototype was first flown on 7 October 1995 and certificated in May 1998 with first deliveries taking place in that month. More than 80 were in service by the end of 2000.

Powerplant: two 15.56-kN (3,500-lb st) Honeywell TFE731-20 turbofans

Performance: max speed 867 km/h (539 mph), cruising speed 846 km/h (526 mph), take-off run 1326 m (4,350 ft); range 3906 km (2,440 miles)

Dimensions: wing span 14.60 m
(47 ft 10 in), length 17.80 m
(58 ft 5 in), height 4.40 m
(14 ft 4 in)

Recognition features
A Two-piece windscreen
B Winglets
C Large ventral fins

Lockheed L-1011 TriStar

The TriStar was Lockheed's contender in the medium-haul wide-body jet airliner market in competition with the DC-10. Like the DC-10 it had three engines, but was designed around the 186.78-kN (42,000 lb st) Rolls-Royce RB.211-22B turbofan. It had capacity for 400 passengers and the prototype flew on 16 November 1970. First deliveries of the L-1011-1 were made in 1972. The L-1011-50 had higher weights, the L-1011-100 had longer-range and the L-1011-200 had higher-thrust RB.211-525B4s. The L-1011-500 TriStar (above) was a 315-passenger long-range version with a shortened fuselage, longer wings and increased fuel capacity. The TriStar line was finally closed in 1983 with delivery of the 250th L-1011, but many examples remain in service.

L-1011-500 TriStar
Powerplant: three 222.40-kN (50,000-lb st) Rolls-Royce RB.211-524B turbofans

Performance: max speed 877 km/h (545 mph), cruising speed 781 km/h (485 mph), initial climb rate 930 m (3,050 ft) per min, range 6896 km (4,310 miles)

Dimensions: wing span 50.09 m
(164 ft 4 in), length 50.04 m
(164 ft 2 in), height 17.02 m
(55 ft 10 in)

Recognition features
A Two wing-mounted engines
B Tail engine exhaust at fuselage
tailcone
C Large-diameter, short-chord
wing nacelles

McDonnell Douglas DC-10/MD-11 *USA*

The DC-10 wide-body, medium-range airliner was designed for the same market as the TriStar. First flown on 29 August 1970, the 380-seat DC-10 had three CF6 turbofans. A total of 138 of the DC-10-10 and DC-10-15 was built. The DC-10-30 and DC-10-40 were long-range versions, 309 of which were completed. This total included 60 KC-10A Extender tankers, based on the convertible DC-10-30CF, for the USAF, and an extended-range DC-10-30ER was also marketed. The DC-10 was re-engineered as the MD-11 (above) which first flew on 10 January 1990. It had a fuselage stretch, modernised flight deck, winglets and a 405-passenger interior. It could be powered by P&W PW4460, Rolls-Royce Trent or CF6-80 engines. MD-11 production ceased in 2001 after 200 had been built including some MD-11F freighters.

DC-10-30ER
Powerplant: three 236.67-kN (53,200-lb st) General Electric CF6-50C2B turbofans

Performance: max speed 950 km/h (594 mph), cruising speed 918 km/h (574 mph), take-off run 3170 m (10,400 ft); range 9760 km (6,100 miles)

Dimensions: wing span 50.39 m
(165 ft 4 in), length 55.35 m
(181 ft 7 in), height 17.70 m
(58 ft 1 in)

Recognition features
A Two wing-mounted engines
B Tail engine exhaust at trailing
edge of fin
C Winglets on MD-11

Piaggio P.180 Avanti   *Italy*

Piaggio's P.180 Avanti twin turboprop business aircraft started as a joint-venture project between Piaggio and Gates Learjet, but Piaggio assumed sole control in January 1986. The P.180, which first flew on 23 September 1986, is a seven- to ten-passenger aircraft of conventional metal construction with a highly streamlined circular-section fuselage and a tricycle undercarriage which retracts into fuselage wells. It has a straight high-aspect-ratio wing set well to the rear of the cabin section, mounting a pair of pusher turboprops driving five-blade Hartzell propellers. Sales of the Avanti have been slow but 38 had been built by the end of 2000 including prototypes and an Italian military batch of eight. The aircraft was relaunched by Piaggio Aero Industries in 1999 and production recommenced to meet outstanding orders for 14 aircraft.

Powerplant: two 1104-kW (1,480-shp) Pratt & Whitney PT6A-66A turboprops

Performance: max speed 732 km/h (455 mph), cruising speed 708 km/h (440 mph), initial climb rate 875 m (2,870 ft) per min, range 3168 km (1,980 miles)

Dimensions: wing span 11.43 m (37 ft 6 in), length 14.40 m (47 ft 3 in), height 3.94 m (12 ft 11 in)

Recognition features
A Sharply-pointed nose with canards
B Twin pusher engines
C T tail

MD Helicopters MD 900 Explorer   *USA*

The MD 900 (right) has a two-crew cockpit and a main cabin with club seating for up to six passengers and a large rear baggage compartment. It is powered by twin P&WC PW206B turboshafts driving a five-blade main rotor. The MD 901 version has twin Arrius 2C turboshafts, while the MD 902 has PW206E engines. The prototype first flew on 18 December 1992.

Recognition features
A Clamshell rear loading doors
B NOTAR tailboom
C Skid U/C

Mooney M.20   *USA*

The four-seat M.20 light aircraft first flew on 10 August 1953, and has been developed into a wide variety of models ranging from the original all-wood M.20, through the M.20B Mark 21 (right) with a tubular frame and metal cladding, to the latest M.20S Eagle. The M.20 remains in production with Mooney Aircraft and around 10,000 had been built by the end of 2001.

Recognition features
A Forward-swept rudder trailing edge
B Low wing
C Retractable, tricycle U/C

Partenavia P.68   *Italy*

Known initially as the 'Victor', the P.68 was first flown on 25 May 1970. Variants range from the initial P.68 with two Lycoming IO-360-A1B engines, through the P.68C-TC with 157-kW (210 hp) turbocharged TIO-360-C1A6Ds to the stretched AP.68TP-600 Viator. The latter is built in 2002 by Vulcanair.

Recognition features
A High wing
B Twin piston engines
C Fixed, tricycle U/C

Pilatus PC-6 Porter

Switzerland

The Porter utility aircraft has been in production since 1960 for roles including cargo hauling, light passenger transport, military STOL operations and parachute dropping. The Porter accommodates up to ten passengers, has wings fitted with high-lift devices for short-field operation and a tailwheel undercarriage. The prototype, which first flew on 4 May 1959, was powered by a 254-kW (340-hp) Lycoming GSO-480-B1A6 piston engine, but a change was made to turboprop power with the PC-6/A-H1 Turbo Porter, first flown in 1961 with a 390-kW (523-shp) Turboméca Astazou IIE. The main versions are the PC-6/B1-H2 (above) with a PT6A-20, the PC-6/B2-H2 and PC-6/B2-H4 and the PC-6/C1-H2 with a Garrett AiResearch TPE331-1-100 which was built under licence by Fairchild Hiller as the Heli-Porter.

PC-6/B2-H4 Turbo Porter
Powerplant: one 507-kW (680-shp) Pratt & Whitney Canada PT6A-27B turboprop

Performance: max speed 266 km/h (165 mph), cruising speed 217 km/h (135 mph), initial climb rate 287 m (940 ft) per min, range 920 km (575 miles)

Dimensions: wing span 15.87 m
(52 ft 1 in), length 10.90 m
(35 ft 9 in), height 3.20 m
(10 ft 6 in)

Recognition features
A Square-section fuselage
B High-wing
C Single engine, turboprops with
very long nose
D Angular fin and rudder

Pilatus PC-12 *Switzerland*

The Pilatus PC-12 (above) (originally referred to as 'PC-XII') first flew on 31 May 1991. It is a multi-purpose utility aircraft. The pressurised fuselage can carry nine passengers and two crew for commuter operations and is fitted with a forward airstair door and a large cargo hatch behind the wing for freight or combi operations. Among PC-12 operators are the Royal Australian Flying Doctor Service, whose aircraft carry two stretcher cases on ambulance flights. Many PC-12s have also been delivered as executive transport or private-owner aircraft. A military variant, the PC-12M Eagle, is available and this is fitted with an underfuselage pod containing surveillance equipment including the Northrop-Grumman WF-160DS dual sensor system. More than 240 PC-12s had been delivered by the end of 2000.

PC-12
Powerplant: one 895-kW (1,200-shp) Pratt & Whitney Canada PT6A-67B turboprop

Performance: max speed 500 km/h (311 mph), cruising speed 463 km/h (288 mph), initial climb rate 512 m (1,680 ft) per min, range 1408 km (880 miles)

Dimensions: wing span 16.23 m
(53 ft 3 in), length 14.40 m
(47 ft 3 in), height 4.27 m (14 ft)

Recognition features
A Single turboprop engine
B T-tail
C Dorsal fin fillet and ventral fins
D Winglets

Piper PA-28 Cherokee, Warrior, Arrow USA

Numerous PA-28 variants have been built since its introduction in 1961. The prototype first flew on 10 January 1960 and minor changes were made during production in the 1960s and 1970s, the aircraft being named Cherokee 160B, Cherokee 180E, etc. Subsequently, the PA-28-180 was given a stretched fuselage as the Challenger and Archer. With the PA-28-151/161 Warrior, Piper added a new semi-tapered wing and stabilator. The Cherokee 235, Charger, Pathfinder and Dakota were higher-powered variants, as was the PA-28-201T Turbo Dakota. The Cherokee Arrow is a retractable-gear version of the PA-28-180 which first flew on 1 February 1966. It progressively incorporated the improvements of other PA-28s, while the Arrow IV (above) has a slimmer rear fuselage and a T-tail with an all-moving tailplane.

PA-28-181 Archer III
Powerplant: one 134-kW (180-hp) Textron Lycoming O-360-A4M piston engine

Performance: max speed 239 km/h (149 mph), cruising speed 222 km/h (138 mph), initial climb rate 203 m (667 ft) per min, range 1069 km (668 miles)

Dimensions: wing span 10.82 m (35 ft 6 in), length 7.31 m (24 ft), height 2.24 m (7 ft 4 in)

Recognition features
A Low wing
B Only Arrow has retractable U/C
C T-tail on Arrow IV

Piper PA-46 Malibu & Malibu Meridian

The Malibu is the only successful pressurised, high-performance single-piston-engined aircraft in production. Its cabin is entered by a port-side rear airstair door and it has standard club-four seating and a two-seat cockpit. The definitive prototype PA-46-310P was first flown on 21 August 1982 and initial production aircraft had a 231-kW (310-hp) Continental TSIO-520-BE turbocharged engine. In 1989 the power was increased with a TIO-540-AE2A and the aircraft redesignated PA-46-350P Malibu Mirage. Piper has used the Mirage airframe to develop the PA-46-400PT Malibu Meridian (above) which is powered by a 298-kW (400-shp) P&WC PT6A-42A turboprop. The first of four prototypes was first flown on 21 August 1998 and the first production Meridians were delivered in 2000.

PA-46-350P Malibu Mirage
Powerplant: one 261-kW (350-hp) Textron Lycoming TIO-540-AE2A piston engine

Performance: max speed 408 km/h (253 mph), cruising speed 395 km/h (245 mph), initial climb rate 371 m (1,218 ft) per min, range 2478 km (1,549 miles)

Dimensions: wing span 13.11 m
(43 ft), length 8.71 m (28 ft 7 in),
height 3.51 m (11 ft 6 in)

Recognition features
A Low, high-aspect ratio wing
B Retractable tricycle U/C
C Turboprop on Meridian
D Rectangular cabin windows

Piper PA-34 Seneca   *USA*

The Seneca six-seat light twin was designed as a larger-capacity companion for the Twin Comanche and was based on the airframe of the PA-32 Cherokee Six. The PA-34-200 Seneca (right), with two 149-kW (200-hp) IO-360 engines was first flown on 20 October 1969. The current production version is the PA-34-220T Seneca V.

Recognition features
A Twin piston engines in long nacelles
B Retractable tricycle U/C

Raytheon 95 Travel Air, 55, 56 & 58 Baron   *USA*

The Beech Model 95 Travel Air was a twin-engined development of the Bonanza. It first flew on 6 August 1956 and was built as the 95, B95, B95A, C95A, D95A and E95. The Model 55 Baron is a Travel Air with a swept tail, longer cabin and IO-470-L engines. The stretched Model 58 (right) remains in production by Raytheon, while Beech also built the pressurised Model 58P. SFERMA developed the SFERMA-60 (PD.146) Marquis with Astazou IIJ turboprops.

Recognition features
A Twin piston engines
B Raised cabin roof line

Robin DR.253, DR.300, DR.400 & DR.500   *France*

On 30 March 1967, the prototype DR.253 Regent was flown as a redesigned, four-seat Jodel DR.250. It was powered by a 134-kW (180 hp) Lycoming O-360-D2A engine and 100 were built. The same airframe was developed into the DR.300 series, the DR.400 and the DR.500 President (right).

Recognition features
A Dihedralled outer wing panels
B Fixed tricycle U/C

Raytheon Beechjet 400

Raytheon acquired the Japanese Mitsubishi MU-300 Diamond business jet in 1985. Mitsubishi flew the original eight-passenger Diamond I prototype for the first time on 29 August 1978. The Diamond II with increased power was also built by Mitsubishi, the company having built 100 Diamonds before production was transferred to Beech at Wichita. The aircraft was renamed Beechjet 400 and received minor cosmetic alterations. The Model 400A is an improved Beechjet with a larger internal cabin and a glass cockpit. The T-1A Jayhawk is a military Model 400A, 180 of which were delivered to the USAF as trainers, and nine Beech 400Ts are in service with the Japanese Air Self Defence Force as trainers.

Beechjet 400A
Powerplant: two 13.19-kN (2,965-lb st) Pratt & Whitney Canada JT15D-5 turbofans

Performance: max speed 867 km/h (539 mph), cruising speed 834 km/h (518 mph), initial climb rate 1150 m (3,770 ft) per min, range 3115 km (1,948 miles)

Dimensions: wing span 13.25 m
(43 ft 6 in), length 14.75 m
(48 ft 5 in), height 4.24 m
(13 ft 11 in)

Recognition features
A T-tail
B Rear-fuselage mounted engine
nacelles
C Short U/C
D Moderately swept wing

Raytheon Hawker Horizon

With the first flight of its super mid-sized, medium-range Hawker Horizon bizjet on 11 August 2001, Raytheon ushered in a new standard in bizjet avionics. The aircraft's Honeywell Primus Epic avionics system introduces capabilities such as full-authority autothrottle control and a moving map display. Voice control of some functions is likely to be a future option. The fuselage employs large composite sections and is aerodynamically advanced, the rear fuselage following the area rule principle to reduce drag around the engine nacelles. The metal wings are built in their entirety by Fuji in Japan, being shipped to Wichita, Kansas for assembly to the fuselage. Seating a maximum of 12 passengers, the Horizon is due for FAA certification in 2003 and is already the subject of at least 150 orders.

Powerplant: two 28.90-kN (6,500-lb st) Pratt & Whitney Canada PW308A turbofans

Performance: (estimated) max operating speed Mach 0.84, take-off run 1600 m (5,250 ft), max certificated altitude 13715 m (45,000 ft), max range 6297 km (3,912 miles)

Dimensions: wing span 18.82 m
(61 ft 9 in), length 21.08 m
(69 ft 2 in), height 5.97 m
(19 ft 7 in)

Recognition features
A 'Waisted' area-ruled rear
fuselage
B T-tail
C Large underfuselage wing root
fairing

Raytheon (Beech) King Air

In 1965 Beech flew the prototype Model 88 development of the earlier Queen Air with a pressurised fuselage, circular windows and IGSO-540 piston engines. By substituting PT6A turboprops, Beech created the Model 90 King Air. The King Air is a six/ eight-seat business aircraft. The A90, B90, C90 and E90 (above) are improved models. The F90 is a high-performance C90 with a T-tail, and other changes. Raytheon currently builds the C90B and C90SE. The stretched Model 100 has a larger fin and 507-kW (680-shp) PT6A-28s. The Super King Air 200, first flown on 27 October 1972, has a T-tail, larger wings, higher weights and more power. The Model 300 has a higher gross weight, yet more power and four-blade propellers, while the stretched Model 350 has winglets.

B200 Super King Air
Powerplant: two 634-kW (850-shp) Pratt & Whitney Canada PT6A-41 turboprops

Performance: max speed 542 km/h (339 mph), cruising speed 520 km/h (325 mph), initial climb rate 747 m (2,450 ft) per minute, range 3320 km (2,075 miles)

Dimensions: wing span 16.60 m
(54 ft 6 in), length 13.36 m
(43 ft 10 in), height 4.53 m
(14 ft 10 in)

Recognition features
A Most models have twin turboprops
B Circular cabin windows
C Later models have T-tail
D Tall undercarriage

Raytheon Premier I

The Premier I was designed by Raytheon to produce an entry-level bizjet slightly smaller than the Beechjet. The Premier I uses composite manufacturing technology and has a filament-wound carbon-fibre and resin honeycomb fuselage and metal wings. The six-passenger Premier I is designed to achieve a long-range cruise speed of Mach 0.80 and a maximum cruising altitude of 12497 m (41,000 ft). The prototype was first flown on 22 December 1998 and five further development aircraft had flown by the end of 2000 with FAA certification being gained on 23 March 2001.

Powerplant: two 10.23-kN (2,300-lb st) Williams FJ44-2A turbofans

Performance: max speed 855 km/h (531 mph), max cruising speed at 10060 m (33,000 ft) 854 km/h (530 mph), take-off run 914 m (3,000 ft), range 2760 km (1,727 miles)

Dimensions: wing span 13.54 m
(44 ft 5 in), length 13.79 m
(45 ft 3 in), height 4.65 m
(15 ft 3 in)

Recognition features
A Three oval cabin windows
B Small size
C T-tail

Robinson R22   *USA*

Robinson's R22 is the most successful light training and personal helicopter in production. It has two side-by-side seats and a two-blade main rotor. The prototype first flew on 28 August 1975. Variants include the R22HP, R22 Alpha (right), R22 Beta, R22 Mariner (with floats) and current-production Beta II. The latter has an O-360 engine derated to 98 kW (131 hp).

Recognition features
A Pod and boom fuselage
B Exposed engine at rear
C Tall main rotor pylon

Robinson R44   *USA*

The four-seat R44 owes much to the R22 and its prototype made its first flight on 31 March 1990. The R44 is unique in being the only production four-seat non-turbine-engined helicopter. Variants include the R44 Astro (right), R44 Raven, R44 Clipper (with large pontoon floats) and R44 Newscopter with gyro-stabilised cameras for electronic news gathering.

Recognition features
A Similar to to R22
B Larger four-seat cabin with four doors
C Engine not exposed

Shorts 330 and 360   *UK*

The 33-passenger SD.330 first flew on 22 August 1974. The SD.330 (later 330-200) was also produced as the military C-23A/B Sherpa for the US, and 330-UTT. The stretched 360 (right) has a single fin. It first flew on 1 June 1981 and variants include the 360-100 and -200, and the -300 with six-blade propellers.

Recognition features
A Main undercarriage in fuselage sponsons
B Square-section fuselage
C Twin vertical tails on 330

Saab 340 and 2000   *Sweden*

In 1979, Saab, in partnership with Fairchild, designed the SF.340 35-passenger, pressurised local service airliner. It was powered by a pair of CT7-5A2 turboprops. The prototype first flew on 25 January 1983. In 1987 Saab took over the whole SF.340 programme and introduced the higher-weight Saab 340B with 1294-kW (1,735-shp) CT7-5A2 (later CT7-9B) engines which was first delivered in September 1989. The Saab 2000 (above, foreground) is a stretched 58-seat model which first flew on 26 March 1992 and is powered by two 3076-kW (4,125-shp) Rolls-Royce AE2100A turboprops with six-blade propellers. In 1997, Saab announced the end of the 340B/2000 production run after 457 340s and 63 2000s had been delivered.

Saab 340B
Powerplant: two 1304-kW (1,750-shp) General Electric CT7-9B turboprops

Performance: max speed 523 km/h (325 mph), cruising speed 512 km/h (318 mph), initial climb rate 610 m (2,000 ft) per minute, range 1676 km (1,048 miles)

Dimensions: wing span 21.44 m
(70 ft 4 in), length 19.73 m
(64 ft 9 in), height 6.96 m
(22 ft 10 in)

Recognition features
A Deep engine nacelles to
accommodate main U/C
B Large dorsal fin and prominent
tailcone
C Dihedralled tailplanes

Scaled Composites Proteus

The Proteus was designed by Burt Rutan's Scaled Composites Inc. as a specialised high-altitude orbiting aircraft to carry communications relay equipment. A fleet of Proteuses may form a relay orbiting system for the Angel Technologies HALO network, carrying podded equipment modules fitted under the centre fuselage. The Model 281 Proteus, which is made primarily from composites, is a tandem-wing aircraft with twin booms and two FJ44 turbofans mounted on the centre section of the rear wing. Its fuselage length can be varied by removal of a section and the wings can be extended asymmetrically if necessary. It is flown by a crew of two in a pressurised cabin and flies above 15240 m (50,000 ft) for 12-hour on-station orbits, although other missions could include military surveillance and a range of mapping and remote-sensing tasks. The prototype first flew on 26 July 1998.

Powerplant: two 10.20-kN (2,293-lb st) Williams FJ44-2E turbofans

Performance: cruising speed 352 km/h (219 mph), initial climb rate 1829 m (6,000 ft) per minute, range 4237 km (2,648 miles)

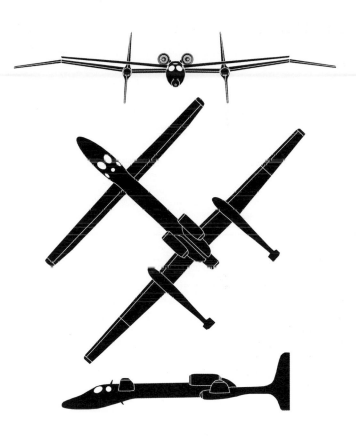

Dimensions: wing span
(standard) 23.65 m (77 ft 7 in),
length (standard) 17.14 m
(56 ft 3 in), height 5.36 m
(17 ft 7 in)

Recognition features
A Unique configuration
B Underfusealge equipment pod
C Drooping nose section

Sino Swearingen SJ30 *USA*

After selling the Merlin business aircraft line to Fairchild, Swearingen Engineering & Technology Inc. designed the SA30 entry-level business jet as a cooperative project, initially with Gulfstream and later with Jaffe Group (as the SJ30). The prototype SJ30 made its first flight on 13 February 1991 and the company was reconstructed in 1995 as Sino Swearingen to build a modified version. The SJ30 is a low-wing six/seven-seat aircraft of primarily metal construction with twin turbofans mounted on the rear fuselage. After initial testing, the prototype SJ30 was rebuilt as the SJ30-2 (above) with a lengthened fuselage, longer wings and higher-rated engines, and it first flew in this form on 8 November 1996. Testing of a new conforming prototype is continuing towards FAR Part 23 certification and 164 orders were in hand by August 2000.

SJ30-2
Powerplant: two 10.23-kN (2,300-lb st) Williams FJ44-2A turbofans

Performance: max speed 980 km/h (609 mph), cruising speed 956 km/h (594 mph), take-off run 1173 m (3,850 ft), range 4603 km (2,877 miles)

Dimensions: wing span 12.90 m
(42 ft 4 in), length 14.30 m
(46 ft 11 in), height 4.34 m
(14 ft 3 in)

Recognition features
A High-aspect ratio swept wing
B Long ventral strakes
C Sharply swept T-tail

SOCATA TBM 700 *France*

Originally launched as a joint project between Aérospatiale and Mooney, the TBM 700 business aircraft was first announced in 1987. It has a two-crew cockpit and a four/five-seat main cabin. The first TBM 700 was flown by SOCATA on 14 July 1988. Mooney subsequently withdrew from the programme and EADS SOCATA now manufactures and markets the aircraft. A total of 160 had been delivered by the end of 2000 and 16 operate with the Armée de l'Air as liaison aircraft. The TBM 700 is offered as a multirole platform for photography, mapping, navaid calibration, etc. and is also being offered as a convertible light freighter with a large port-side freight door and hardened interior.

TBM 700
Powerplant: one 522-kW (700-shp) (derated) Pratt & Whitney Canada PT6A-64 turboprop

Performance: max speed 555 km/h (345 mph), cruising speed 450 km/h (280 mph), initial climb rate 725 m (2,380 ft) per minute, range 2870 km (1,795 miles)

Dimensions: wing span 12.68 m
(41 ft 7 in), length 10.64 m
(34 ft 11 in), height 4.35 m
(14 ft 3 in)

Recognition features
A Single turboprop
B Twin nose jetpipes
C Usually has podded weather
radar on port wing leading edge

Sukhoi Su-26, Su-29 and Su-31 *Russia*

The low-wing Su-26 is an advanced competition aerobatic aircraft.
The Su-26M is a sophisticated design of steel tube and titanium with
a composite wing and aluminium and composite cladding. It is a
single-seater with an M-14P engine. The prototype flew in June 1984.
The Su-26MX is stressed to higher limits with increased fuel capacity,
and the Su-31, which replaced the Su-26, has a stretched fuselage and
longer wings, a higher-powered M-14PF engine, a taller undercarriage,
a cut-down rear fuselage and a modified side-hinged bubble canopy.
The Su-29 (above) is a stretched tandem two-seat version of the Su-31.
Sukhoi has also tested a special Su-29LL model with twin ejection
seats.

Su-29
Powerplant: one 268-kW
(360-hp) Vedeneyev M-14P
piston engine

Performance: max speed
325 km/h (202 mph), cruising
speed 314 km/h (195 mph), initial
climb rate 960 m (3,150 ft) per
minute, range 1200 km
(750 miles)

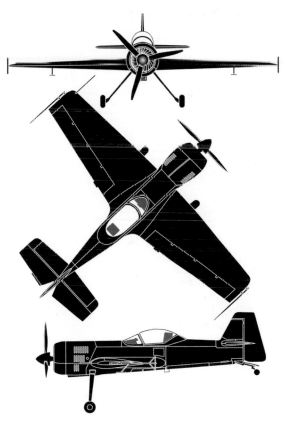

Dimensions: wing span 8.20 m
(26 ft 11 in), length 7.32 m (24 ft),
height 2.88 m (9 ft 6 in)

Recognition features
A Large radial piston engine
B Simple fixed tailwheel U/C

Sikorsky S-76 Spirit   *USA*

The prototype S-76 first flew on 13 March 1977. It is a 12-passenger high-performance executive and light transport helicopter. The standard S-76 has two 485-kW (650-shp) Rolls-Royce 250-C30 turboshafts driving a four-blade main rotor. Variants include the S-76 Mk II, S-76A, S-76B, Arriel 1S1-powered S-76C and S-76C+ (right). Early S-76s re-engined with Arriels are designated S-76A+.

Recognition features
A No ventral fin
B Retractable tricycle U/C
C No tailcone

Sikorsky S-92 Helibus   *USA*

The Helibus medium-lift multi-role helicopter is aimed at both military and civil markets, with a 19/ 22-passenger cabin. It has a two-crew cockpit and a dynamic system based on that of the S-70. It is powered by two 1306-kW (1,750 shp) GE CT7-8 turboshafts which are mounted either side of the main rotor pylon. The first S-92 flew on 23 December 1998.

Recognition features
A Rear ramp
B Large fuselage sponsons for baggage, fuel and U/C
C Four-blade rotors

SOCATA TB 9 Tampico and TB 10 Tobago   *France*

In April 1977 the first of the new TB series of four-seaters was flown. This entered production as the TB 9 Tampico and TB 10 Tobago with 119-kW (160-hp) and 134-kW (180-hp) engines respectively. Versions include the TB 9C Tampico Club, TB 200 Tobago XL (right), TB 9NG (Nouvelle Génération) and TB 10NG. The type remains in production by EADS SOCATA.

Recognition features
A Low wing
B High cabin roof line

Tupolev Tu-204

Russia

Tupolev's replacement for the medium-haul Tu-154 is the Tu-204, which was initiated in 1983. It is a twin-turbofan 200-passenger aircraft, competitive with the Boeing 757. The prototype made its maiden flight on 2 January 1989, but Russian type certification was not achieved until six years later. Sales of the Tu-204 have been hampered by lack of customer finance. Other versions of the Tu-204 include the long-range Tu-204-100 (above) and Tu-204-100C combi, Tu-204-120 with Rolls-Royce RB.211-535E4 engines, and Tu-204C freighter with a forward port cargo door. The Tu-204-200 (also known as the Tu-214) has a higher gross weight with increased fuel capacity, and is also available in -200C combi and RB.211 Tu-204-220 versions. Tupolev has also built a prototype of the Tu-234 which was announced in 1995 and has a 5.79-m (19-ft) shorter fuselage and 166 seats.

Tu-204-100
Powerplant: two 158.30-kN (35,582-lb st) Aviadvigatel-Perm PS-90A turbofans

Performance: max speed 853 km/h (530 mph), cruising speed 806 km/h (501 mph), range 4872 km (3,045 miles)

Dimensions: wing span 42.01 m
(137 ft 10 in), length 46 m
(150 ft 11 in), height 13.89 m
(45 ft 7 in)

Recognition features
A Winglets
B Long chord of PS-90 nacelles

Tupolev Tu-334

Tupolev designed the Tu-334 short-haul airliner as a replacement for the Tu-134 on routes of up to 3058 km (1,900 miles). With 102-passenger capacity the Tu-334 has a low wing with winglets and twin Progress D-436T turbofans mounted on the rear fuselage. The Tu-334-100 prototype was rolled out in 1995 but not flown until 8 February 1999 as a result of insufficient funding. Certification had still not been achieved at the start of 2002, but many variants are planned. These include a Westernised version, the Tu-334-120, with Rolls-Royce Deutschland BR710-48 turbofans, although Rolls-Royce Deutschland is only likely to support future versions with more-powerful BR715s; Tu-334-100C combi; the extended-range Tu-334-100M and the stretched 126-seat Tu-334-200 (also known as the Tu-354).

Tu-334-100
Powerplant: two 73.55-kN (16,535-lb st) Progress D-436T turbofans

Performance: max speed 821 km/h (510 mph), cruising speed 797 km/h (495 mph), range 1800 km (1,125 miles)

Dimensions: wing span 29.77 m
(97 ft 8 in), length 17.83 m
(58 ft 6 in), height 5.21 m
(17 ft 1 in)

Recognition features
A Broad-chord fin
B Deep fuselage
C Short undercarriage

Wolfsburg-Evektor Raven
Czech Republic

Designed by Alec Clark of Wolfsburg Aircraft, the Raven is a twin piston-engined utility aircraft aimed at the market served by the Britten-Norman Islander but offering greater internal capacity and ease of loading for palletised cargo and 'D' Type containers. It is of all-metal construction and has a twin boom layout, a fixed tricycle undercarriage and a square section fuselage with large rear loading and side loading doors. It can be fitted with eight main-cabin passenger seats or can be used as a freighter, for parachuting or in aeromedical configuration. The prototype first flew on 28 July 2000 and it is being developed, and should be built in quantity, by Evektor-Aerotechnik of Kunovice in the Czech Republic.

Raven 257
Powerplant: two 224-kW (300-hp) Teledyne Continental IO-550-N piston engines

Performance: max speed 268 km/h (167 mph), cruising speed 240 km/h (149 mph), initial climb rate 450 m (1,476 ft) per minute, range 1325 km (828 miles)

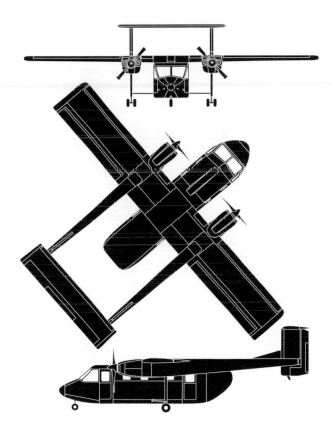

Dimensions: wing span 14 m
(45 ft 11 in), length 12.29 m
(40 ft 4 in), height 3.99 m
(13 ft 1 in)

Recognition features
A Twin tail booms
B High-set, bridge tailplane
C High wing
D Rounded rear fuselage

Yakovlev Yak-42 'Clobber' *Russia*

The Yak-42 (NATO 'Clobber') was developed as a replacement for the Il-18 and Tu-134 in regional service in the USSR. It has seating for 120 passengers, and Yakovlev followed the low-wing layout of its successful Yak-40. The swept-wing Yak-42 has a conventional retractable tricycle undercarriage with four-wheel main bogies for landing on poorer remote airfields. The prototype first flew on 7 March 1975. The current Yak-42D (above) has additional fuel, the Yak-42A is a combi passenger/freight aircraft and the Yak-42F is a geophysical survey version. New or projected versions include the Yak-42D-90 which has an increased fuel load but reduced 90-passenger seating. Production of the Yak-42 at Saratov is believed to be around 200 aircraft to date, and the type is widely used by foreign airlines and those serving the former Aeroflot domestic network.

Yak-42D
Powerplant: three 63.70-kN (14,330-lb st) Lotarev D-36 turbofans

Performance: max speed 810 km/h (503 mph), cruising speed 750 km/h (466 mph), range 2200 km (1,375 miles)

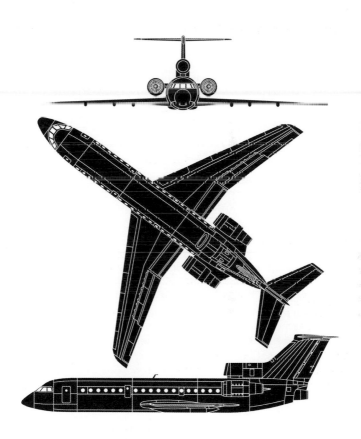

Dimensions: wing span 34.88 m
(114 ft 5 in), length 36.38 m
(119 ft 5 in), height 9.83 m
(32 ft 4 in)

Recognition features
A T-tail
B Tail engine exhaust at fuselage
tailcone

Swearingen Merlin and Metro   *USA*

The SA-26 Merlin IIA executive aircraft first flew on 13 April 1965. Five SA-26 variants were built, while stretching the SA-226T Merlin III (right) produced the 20-seat SA-226T Metro airliner. Variants included the executive SA-226AT Merlin IV, SA-226TC Metro II, SA-227AC Metro III, Expediter freighter, executive SA-227AT Merlin IVC and SA-227DC Metro 23 with optional belly pannier.

Recognition features
A Low wing
B Stalky U/C
C Long, narrow fuselage of Metro

Yakovlev Yak-50 & Yak-52   *Russia*

The Yak-50 single-seat competition aerobatic aircraft was designed for the 1976 World Aerobatic Championships. It used a similar fuselage to that of the earlier Yak-18PS but with a new wing. It had a retractable tailwheel U/C and an M-14P radial. The Yak-52 (right) was developed as a tandem two-seat basic trainer with retractable tricycle U/C. The type remains in production by Aerostar in Romania.

Recognition features
A Large radial engine
B Rounded vertical tail

Zlin Z 42 to Z 242   *Czech Republic*

The original Z 41 had a low, slightly forward-swept wing, two seats and fixed tricycle U/C. The subsequent production Z 42 was first flown on 17 October 1967. Variants included the Z 42M, Z 142 (right) and Z 242L. The Z 43 is a four-seater with a lengthened fuselage. The four-seat Z 143L was developed from the Z 142.

Recognition features
A Angular flying surfaces
B Clear-vision canopy on Z 142

Aviation as a Hobby

Aircraft are exciting! Next to computers, aviation is probably the technology which has most changed the world in the twentieth century. Airlife invites you to discover the Aviation Hobby – which provides a fascination to many thousands of people around the globe.

Identifying different types of aircraft became important in World War I – and a matter of life and death in World War II. Britain, which was on the front line of wartime Luftwaffe attacks, set up spotting posts along its Channel Coast and this emphasis on 'spotting' continued after the war with the Royal Observer Corps – and is kept alive with the present-day hobby carried on by aircraft enthusiasts around the globe. The aircraft spotting habit has expanded into a wide-ranging interest which includes aircraft recognition, collection of aircraft registrations, photography, research into aircraft production and the detailed study of aircraft and aviation history.

Aircraft Recognition

For the casual observer, one aircraft can be almost indistinguishable from another. The problem becomes more complicated rather than less as new aircraft types are added to our crowded skies. The number of types of aircraft has grown rapidly during the 1980s and 1990s and competing designers have often come up with very similar answers to particular specifications. Until one has mastered the art of aircraft recognition, a DC-10 and a TriStar can be easily confused – and separating a Saab Gripen from a Eurofighter or Dassault Rafale in a high-speed flying display can test even the most expert observer.

To become a recognition expert there is no substitute for experience. The enthusiast will quickly become conversant with different aircraft types by reading aviation magazines, visiting airports and going to airshows. However, there are some essential guidelines which will speed up the process of identification.

First impressions are always the most important. An aircraft flies overhead and one should be able to tell immediately whether it is large or small. Does it look like an airliner, a light aircraft, a helicopter, a military jet – or even a glider? Can you tell from the noise it makes whether it is powered by jet or piston engines? These are judgements which nearly everyone can make and they immediately narrow down the range of possible answers. Sometimes, the solution comes easily. You can visit an airport where there are confusing rows of airliners – but many of them will have 'Boeing 777' or 'Airbus 320' painted on the side, which solves the problem immediately.

Once the initial judgement is made, you can start to look at the general characteristics of the aircraft. Cast your eyes over its main components and mentally list its features.

The wings
- are they High, Mid or Low set on the fuselage?
- are there one (monoplane), two (biplane) or, maybe, three (triplane) sets of wings?
- are they straight wings, swept – or maybe delta-shaped?

The engines
- how many engines does the aircraft have?
- are they propeller-driven or jet engines?
- if there are two or more engines, are they mounted on the wings or on the fuselage?

The tail
- does it have a single fin – or two or three fins – or, maybe, a V-tail?
- is it swept back or 'straight'?
- does it have the tailplane positioned at the top, middle or the base?

The fuselage (the body of the aircraft)
- does it have a conventional fuselage or does it have twin booms?
- what kind of cabin does it have? A bubble cockpit, an open cockpit, or a large flight deck?
- is the rear fuselage continuous or upswept (perhaps with a cargo ramp)?
- are there cabin windows along the fuselage?
- what does the landing gear look like? Is it fixed or retractable, tricycle or tailwheel?
- if it is a military jet, where is the air intake – in the nose, flanking the cockpit area, etc?

If in doubt, write down your conclusions before you search through the pages of this book to find out which type you have seen. Your summary may say – 'Large airliner with swept back low wings, four engines fitted under the wings, tailplane attached to the fuselage and a retracting tricycle undercarriage'.

Or – 'Single-seat jet fighter with one engine and delta wings'. Or even – 'High-wing light aircraft with a single propeller-driven engine in the nose and a fixed tricycle undercarriage'.

This technique will allow you to eliminate the vast majority of aircraft – but it will leave you with a short list of types which look dauntingly similar. This is the point at which you have to get down to the fine differences leading to a correct identification. Do not worry if you cannot reach the answer immediately. Even experienced spotters find difficulty with, for instance, the wide-body Boeing 767 and Boeing 777 when seen at a distance. Here it is necessary to look very closely at the competing types and find the tiny differences. In the case of the wide-body Boeings, for instance, the '777 is larger than the '767 – but that may not be evident if you cannot see the two parked side-by-side! However, the '777 has a distinctive squared-off tail cone on its fuselage whereas the '767 tailcone is pointed – and the main undercarriage of the '777 has six wheels on each bogie, whereas the '767 has four.

Regrettably, even with this close scrutiny the enthusiast can come to the wrong conclusion. Most successful aircraft types are produced in different versions to meet various requirements. It is very common for airliner types to be 'stretched' so as to accommodate varying passenger loads. For instance, Boeing's highly successful '737 started out as the Model 100 with a 94-ft fuselage capable of carrying up to 101 passengers but has expanded to the 177-seat '737-900 which is 138-ft long. A useful distinguishing feature separating the Airbus A320 and the Boeing 737 was the winglets fitted to the Airbus; unfortunately, recent Boeing 737s have also had winglets added! So, the enthusiast has to accumulate experience and familiarity with all these aircraft – and also resort to a range of other methods of identification.

Aircraft Registrations

Both civil and military aircraft carry individual registration markings. In the case of civil aircraft these include a national identification consisting of one or two prefix letters which are issued by the International Civil Aviation Organisation (ICAO). A full listing of these prefixes is given in this book. The military authorities of each country also allocate their own serial numbers and use a system of distinctive national markings (which are shown in Airlife's *Military Aircraft Recognition*). Civil and military registrations for most countries in the world are given in a variety of commercially available directories which can be purchased by enthusiasts.

There are also annual volumes which concentrate on particular classes of aircraft – such as business jets, and there are many websites on the internet which can be accessed through index sites such as tgplanes or AirNet. Clearly, it is a simple matter to identify an aircraft's type by noting its registration and checking its details in one of these directories. In addition, many civil aircraft registers provide details of the owner of the aircraft, which adds to the interest of spotting the aircraft.

The directories also give details of the manufacturer's serial number (the 'construction number' or 'c/n') which gives a good idea of where the aircraft falls within the overall production of that model. The c/n is also useful for identifying an aircraft which has changed registration. This will happen when an aircraft is sold from one country to another and is allocated new markings by its new country of ownership.

Many aircraft enthusiasts keep a log of all the aircraft they have seen. It is, of course, impossible to see and log every aircraft in the world! So, most spotters concentrate on particular types or classes of aircraft with the objective of seeing and logging them all. One may collect business jets or airliners – or military aircraft. A pair of binoculars are very helpful – and a good notebook is essential. This can be a proprietary notebook such as *Airlife's Aircraft Logbook* or a simple lined notebook is more than adequate when ruled with columns showing the place and date seen, the registration and aircraft type. Other details may include the airline or operator and information on the colour scheme or special markings. Some spotters collect every different registration – and some are happy if they log a particular airframe irrespective of the registration it is carrying. The choice is an individual one.

Books and Magazines

The range of books and magazines is enormous and the only limitation is the size of your bank balance! Weekly magazines such as *Flight International* and *Aviation Week* cater primarily for those in the aviation industry while many monthly magazines are published for enthusiasts. These include *Aeroplane Monthly*, *Air Pictorial*, *Flypast*, *Pilot* and *Air International* in the UK and *Flying*, *Private Pilot* and *Air & Space* in the US. Books are available on almost every aviation subject and the large range of Airlife titles can be viewed and purchased at www.airlifebooks.com. We hope you enjoy discovering the exciting world of aircraft!

International Aircraft Registration Prefixes by Country

Country	Prefix	Country	Prefix
Afghanistan	YA	Central African Rep.	TL
Algeria	7T	Chad	TT
Angola	D2	Chile	CC
Anguilla	VP-A	China	B
Antigua & Barbuda	V2	Colombia	HK
Argentina	LQ, LV	Congo	TN
Armenia	EK	Congo, Dem. Rep.	9Q
Aruba	P4	Costa Rica	TI
Australia	VH	Côte d'Ivoire	TU
Austria	OE	Croatia	9A
Azerbaijan	4K	Cuba	CU
Bahamas	C6	Cyprus	5B
Bahrain	A9C	Czech Republic	OK
Bangladesh	S2	Denmark	OY
Barbados	8P	Djibouti	J2
Belarus	EW	Dominica	J7
Belgium	OO	Dominican Rep.	HI
Belize	V3	Ecuador	HC
Benin	TY	Egypt	SU
Bermuda	VP-B	El Salvador	YS
Bhutan	A5	Equatorial Guinea	3C
Bolivia	CP	Estonia	ES
Bosnia-Herzegovina	T9	Ethiopia	ET
Botswana	A2	Falkland Islands	VP-F
Brazil	PP, PT	Fiji	DQ
Brunei	V8	Finland	OH
Bulgaria	LZ	France	F
Burkina Faso	XT	Gabon	TR
Burundi	9U	Gambia	C5
Cambodia	XU	Georgia	4L
Cameroon	TJ	Germany	D
Canada	C, CF	Ghana	9G
Cape Verde	D4	Gibraltar	VP-G
Cayman Islands	VP-C	Greece	SX

Grenada	J3	Malaysia	9M
Guatemala	TG	Maldives	8Q
Guinea	3X	Mali	TZ
Guinea Bissau	J5	Malta	9H
Guyana	8R	Marshall Islands	V7
Haiti	HH	Mauretania	5T
Honduras	HR	Mauritius	3B
Hong Kong	B-H	Mexico	XA, VB, XC
Hungary	HA	Micronesia	V6
Iceland	TF	Moldova	ER
India	VT	Monaco	3A
Indonesia	PK	Montserrat	VP-M
Iran	EP	Mozambique	C9
Iraq	YI	Myanmar	XY, XZ
Ireland	EI, EJ	Namibia	V5
Israel	4X	Nauru	C2
Italy	I	Nepal	9N
Jamaica	6Y	Netherlands	PH
Japan	JA	Netherlands Antilles	PJ
Jordan	JY	New Zealand	ZK
Kazakhstan	UN	Nicaragua	YN
Kenya	5Y	Niger	5U
Korea, North	P	Nigeria	5N
Korea, South	HL	Norway	LN
Kuwait	9K	Oman	A4O
Kyrgyzstan	EX	Pakistan	AP
Laos	RDPL	Panama	HP
Latvia	YL	Papua New Guinea	P2
Lebanon	OD	Paraguay	ZP
Lesotho	7P	Peru	OB
Liberia	EL	Philippines	RP
Libya	5A	Poland	SP
Liechtenstein	HB	Portugal	CR, CS
Lithuania	LY	Qatar	A7
Luxembourg	LX	Romania	YR
Macedonia	Z3	Russian Fed.	RA
Madagascar	5R	Rwanda	9XR
Malawi	7QY	Samoa	5W

San Marino	T7	Tanzania	5H
Sao Tome & Principe	S9	Thailand	HS
Saudi Arabia	HZ	Togo	5V
Senegal	6V, 6W	Tonga	A3
Seychelles	S7	Trinidad & Tobago	9Y
Sierra Leone	9L	Tunisia	TS
Singapore	9V	Turkey	TC
Slovakia	OM	Turkmenistan	EZ
Slovenia	S5	Turks & Caicos	VQ-T
Solomon Islands	H4	Uganda	5X
Somalia	6O	Ukraine	UR
South Africa	ZS, ZT, ZU	United Arab Emirates	A6
Spain	EC	United Kingdom	G
Sri Lanka	4R	United States	N
St. Kitts & Nevis	V4	Uruguay	CX
St. Lucia	J6	Uzbekistan	UK
St. Vincent & Grenadines	J8	Vanuatu	YJ
St. Helena/Ascension	VQ-H	Venezuela	YV
Sudan	ST	Vietnam	XV
Surinam	PZ	Virgin Islands	VP-L
Swaziland	3D	Yemen	7O
Sweden	SE	Yugoslavia	YU
Switzerland	HB	Zaire	9Q
Syria	YK	Zambia	9J
Taiwan	B-	Zimbabwe	Z
Tajikistan	EY		

International Aircraft Registration Mark Prefixes

A2	Botswana	EW	Belarus
A3	Tonga	EX	Kyrgyzstan
A4O	Oman	EY	Tajikistan
A5	Bhutan	EZ	Turkmenistan
A6	United Arab	F	France
	Emirates	G	United Kingdom
A7	Qatar	H4	Solomon Islands
A9C	Bahrain	HA	Hungary
AP	Pakistan	HB	Liechtenstein
B	China	HB	Switzerland
B-	Taiwan	HC	Ecuador
B-H	Hong Kong	HH	Haiti
C2	Nauru	HI	Dominican Rep.
C5	Gambia	HK	Colombia
C6	Bahamas	HL	Korea, South
C9	Mozambique	HP	Panama
CC	Chile	HR	Honduras
CP	Bolivia	HS	Thailand
CR, CS	Portugal	HZ	Saudi Arabia
CU	Cuba	I	Italy
CX	Uruguay	J2	Djibouti
C, CF	Canada	J3	Grenada
D	Germany	J5	Guinea Bissau
D2	Angola	J6	St. Lucia
D4	Cape Verde	J7	Dominica
DQ	Fiji	J8	St. Vincent &
EC	Spain		Grenadines
EI, EJ	Ireland	JA	Japan
EK	Armenia	JY	Jordan
EL	Liberia	LN	Norway
EP	Iran	LQ, LV	Argentina
ER	Moldova	LX	Luxembourg
ES	Estonia	LY	Lithuania
ET	Ethiopia	LZ	Bulgaria

N	United States	TR	Gabon
OB	Peru	TS	Tunisia
OD	Lebanon	TT	Chad
OE	Austria	TU	Côte d'Ivoire
OH	Finland	TY	Benin
OK	Czech Republic	TZ	Mali
OM	Slovakia	UK	Uzbekistan
OO	Belgium	UN	Kazakhstan
OY	Denmark	UR	Ukraine
P	Korea, North	V2	Antigua & Barbuda
P2	Papua New Guinea	V3	Belize
P4	Aruba	V4	St. Kitts & Nevis
PH	Netherlands	V5	Namibia
PJ	Netherlands Antilles	V6	Micronesia
PK	Indonesia	V7	Marshall Islands
PP, PT	Brazil	V8	Brunei
PZ	Surinam	VH	Australia
RA	Russian Fed.	VP-A	Anguilla
RDPL	Laos	VP-B	Bermuda
RP	Philippines	VP-C	Cayman Islands
S2	Bangladesh	VP-F	Falkland Islands
S5	Slovenia	VP-G	Gibraltar
S7	Seychelles	VP-L	Virgin Islands
S9	Sao Tome & Principe	VP-M	Montserrat
SE	Sweden	VQ-H	St. Helena/Ascension
SP	Poland	VQ-T	Turks & Caicos
ST	Sudan	VT	India
SU	Egypt	XA, VB, XC	Mexico
SX	Greece	XT	Burkina Faso
T7	San Marino	XU	Cambodia
T9	Bosnia-Herzegovina	XV	Vietnam
TC	Turkey	XY, XZ	Myanmar
TF	Iceland	YA	Afghanistan
TG	Guatemala	YI	Iraq
TI	Costa Rica	YJ	Vanuatu
TJ	Cameroon	YK	Syria
TL	Central African Rep.	YL	Latvia
TN	Congo	YN	Nicaragua

YR	Romania	5X	Uganda
YS	El Salvador	5Y	Kenya
YU	Yugoslavia	6O	Somalia
YV	Venezuela	6V, 6W	Senegal
Z	Zimbabwe	6Y	Jamaica
Z3	Macedonia	7O	Yemen
ZK	New Zealand	7P	Lesotho
ZP	Paraguay	7QY	Malawi
ZS, ZT, ZU	South Africa	7T	Algeria
3A	Monaco	8P	Barbados
3B	Mauritius	8Q	Maldives
3C	Equatorial Guinea	8R	Guyana
3D	Swaziland	9A	Croatia
3X	Guinea	9G	Ghana
4K	Azerbaijan	9H	Malta
4L	Georgia	9J	Zambia
4R	Sri Lanka	9K	Kuwait
4X	Israel	9L	Sierra Leone
5A	Libya	9M	Malaysia
5B	Cyprus	9N	Nepal
5H	Tanzania	9Q	Congo, Dem. Rep.
5N	Nigeria	9Q	Zaire
5R	Madagascar	9U	Burundi
5T	Mauretania	9V	Singapore
5U	Niger	9XR	Rwanda
5V	Togo	9Y	Trinidad & Tobago
5W	Samoa		

Principal Airlines of the World

Aer Lingus	EI	America West	HP
Aero California	JR	American A/L	AA
Aero Lloyd	YP	Am. Trans Air	TZ
Aeroflot	SU	AOM Airlines	IW
Aerolineas Argentinas	AR	Arkia Israeli	IZ
Aeromexico	AM	Armenian A/L	R3
Aeropostal Venezuela	VH	Arrow Air	JW
Air 2000	DP	Asiana	OZ
Air Algerie	AH	Atlant-Soyuz	3G
Air Atlanta	CC	Atlas Air	5Y
Air Berlin	AB	Augsburg A/W	IQ
Air Botswana	BP	Aurigny Air Serv.	GR
Air Canada	AC	Austrian A/L	OS
Air China	CA	AVIANCA	AV
Air Europa	UX	Azerbaijan A/L	J2
Air France	AF	Bahamasair	UP
Air India	AI	Balkan Bulgarian	LZ
Air Jamaica	JM	Belavia	B2
Air Kazakhstan	9Y	Biman Bangladesh	BG
Air Malta	KM	Braathens	BU
Air Nippon	EL	Brit Air	DB
Air New Zealand	NZ	Britannia Airways	BY
Air Nostrum	YW	British Airways	BA
Air Seychelles	HM	British European	JY
Air Transat	TS	British Mediterranean	KJ
Air Ukraine	6U	British Midland	BD
Air Zimbabwe	UM	British Regional	TH
Airborne Express	GB	BWIA	BW
Airtours Int.	VZ	Canada 3000	2T
Airtran A/W	FL	Canadian Regional	KI
Alaska Airlines	AS	Cargolux	CV
Alitalia	AZ	Cathay Pacific	CX
All Nippon	NH	China Airlines	CI
Aloha Airlines	AQ	China Eastern	MU

China Northern	CJ	Iberia	IB
China Southern	CZ	Icelandair	FI
CityFlyer Express	FD	Indian A/L	IC
Condor Flugdienst	DE	Iran Air	IR
Continental A/L	CO	Iraqi Airways	IA
Croatia A/L	OU	Japan Air System	JD
Crossair	LX	Japan Airlines	JL
Cubana	CU	JAT	JU
Cyprus A/W	CY	Jersey European	JY
Czech Airlines	OK	Jet Airways	9W
Dalavia	H8	JetBlue Airways	B6
Delta Air Lines	DL	IMC Air	MT
Deutsche BA	DI	Kenya A/W	KQ
DHL Airways	ER	KLM	KL
Domodedovo A/L	E3	KLM Express	WA
Dragonair	KA	Korean A/L	KE
Druk Air	KB	Kras Air	7B
easyJet	U2	Kuwait Airways	KU
Egyptair	MS	Kyrghyzstan A/L	K2
El Al Israel	LY	LAN-Chile	LA
Emery Worldwide	EB	LAPA	MJ
Emirates	EK	Lauda Air	L4
Estonian Air	OV	LIAT	LI
Ethiopian Airlines	ET	Libyan Arab	LN
European Aviation	E7	Lloyd Aero Boliviano	LB
Eurowings	EW	LOT Polish A/L	LO
EVA Air	BR	LTU International	LT
Evergreen Int.	EZ	Lufthansa	LH
Federal Express	FX	Lufthansa Cityline	CL
Finnair	AY	Luxair	LG
Frontier A/L	F9	Maersk Air	DM
Garuda	GA	Malaysia A/L	MH
GO	OG	Malév Hungary	MA
Gulf Air	GF	Martinair	MP
Gulfstream Int.	3M	Meridiana	IG
Hapag-Lloyd	HF	Merpati Nusantara	MZ
Hawaiian A/L	HA	Mexicana	MX
Horizon A/L	QX	MIAT-Mongolian	OM

Midwest Express	YX	Sun Country	SY
Monarch A/L	ZB	Swissair	SR
Northwest A/L	NW	Syrianair	RB
Olympic Airways	OA	TAAG Angola	DT
Pakistan Int.	PK	TACA International	TA
Pelita Air Service	EP	Tajik Air	7J
Philippine A/L	PR	TAM Brazil	KK
PLUNA	PU	TAP Air Portugal	TP
Polar Air Cargo	POP	Tarom	RO
Portugalia	NI	Thai Airways Int.	TG
Qantas Airways	QF	TNT Airways	3V
Qatar Airways	Q7	Transavia A/L	HV
Regional Airlines	VM	Tunisair	TU
Rio-Sul	SL	Turkish A/L	TK
Royal Air Maroc	AT	United A/L	UA
Royal Jordanian	RJ	United Parcel Service	5X
Ryanair	FR	US Airways	US
SAS	SK	Uzbekistan A/W	HY
Saudi Arabian	SV	Vanguard A/L	NJ
Sibir A/L	5M	Varig	RG
Singapore A/L	SQ	VASP	VP
Skywest	OO	Virgin Atlantic	VS
South African A/W	SA	Virgin Blue	DJ
Southwest A/L	WN	Vnukovo A/L	V5
Spanair	JK	Wideroes Flyveselskap	WF
Spirit A/L	NK	World Airways	WO
Sterling European	NB		

Codes for Principal Airports

U.K. Airports

Aberdeen	EGPD	ABZ
Belfast	EGAA	BFS
Blackpool	EGNH	BLK
Birmingham	EGBB	BHM
Bournemouth	EGHH	BOH
Bristol	EGGD	BRS
Cambridge	EGSC	CBG
Cardiff	EGFF	CWL
Carlisle	EGNC	CAX
Cranfield	EGTC	
Dundee	EGPN	DND
Edinburgh	EGPH	EDI
Exeter	EGTE	EXT
E. Midlands	EGNX	EMA
Farnborough	EGUF	
Gatwick	EGKK	LGW
Glasgow	EGPF	GLA
Heathrow	EGLL	LHR
Humberside	EGNJ	HUY
Inverness	EGPE	INV
Leeds/Bradford	EGNM	LBA
Liverpool	EGGP	LPL
London City	EGLC	LCY
Luton	EGGW	LTN
Manchester	EGGC	MAN
Newcastle	EGNT	NCL
Norwich	EGSH	NWI
Plymouth	EGHD	PLH
Prestwick	EGPK	PIK
Southampton	EGHI	SOU
Southend	EGMC	SEN
Stansted	EGSS	STN
Teeside	EGNV	MME

Continental Europe

Amsterdam	EHAM	AMS
Ankara	LTAC	ESB
Athens	LGAT	ATH
Barcelona	LEBL	BCN
Belgrade	LEBL	BCN
Berlin	ETBS	SXF
Brussels	EBBR	BRU
Bucharest	LRBB	BUH
Budapest	LHBP	BUD
Copenhagen	EKCH	CPH
Dublin	EIDW	DUB
Dusseldorf	EDOL	DUS
Franfurt	EDDF	FRA
Geneva	LSGG	GVA
Hamburg	EDOH	HAM
Helsinki	EFHF	HEM
Lisbon	LPPT	LIS
Madrid	LEMD	MAD
Malta	LMML	MLA
Milan	LIMC	MXP
Moscow	UUEE	SVO
Munich	EDDM	MUC
Nice	LFMN	NCE
Oslo	ENGM	GEN
Paris-CDG	LFPG	CDG
Paris-Orly	LFPO	ORY
Prague	LKPR	PRG
Rome	LIRA	CIA
Stockholm	ESSA	ARN
Turin	LIMF	TRN
Vienna	LOWW	VIE
Warsaw	EPWA	WAW
Zurich	LSZH	ZRH

United States and Canada

Anchorage, AK	PANC	ANC
Atlanta, GA	KATL	ATL
Boston, MA	KBOS	BOS
Charleston, SC	KCHS	CHS
Chicago, IL	KORD	CHI
Cleveland, OH	KCLE	CLE
Dallas, TX	KDFW	DFW
Denver, CO	KDEN	DEN
Detroit, MI	KDET	DTT
Houston, TX	KHOU	HOU
Kansas City, MO	KMCI	MKC
Los Angeles, CA	KLAX	LAX
Memphis, TN	KMEM	MEM
Miami, FL	KMIA	MIA
Minneapolis, MN	KMSP	MSP
Montreal	CYMX	YMQ
New Orleans, LA	KMSY	MSY
New York – JFK	KJFK	JFK
Newark, NJ	KEWR	EWR
Philadelphia, PA	KPHL	PHL
Phoenix, AZ	KPHX	PHX
Las Vegas, NV	KLAS	LAS
Pittsburg, PA	KPIT	PIT
Raleigh-Durham, NC	KRDU	RDU
Salt Lake City, UT	KSLC	SLC
San Franscisco, CA	KSFO	SFO
Seattle, WA	KSEA	SEA
St. Louis, MO	KSTL	STL
Tampa, FL	KTPA	TPA
Toronto	CYYZ	YTO
Vancouver	CYVR	YVR
Washington Dulles	KIAD	WAS
Winnipeg	CYWG	YWG

Latin America and the Caribbean

Acapulco	MMAA	ACA
Antigua	TAPA	ANU
Asuncion	SGAS	ASU
Barbados	TBPB	BGI
Belize City	MZBZ	BZE
Bermuda	TXKF	BDA
Bogota	SKED	BOG
Brasilia	SBBR	BSB
Buenos Aires	SABA	BUE
Caracas	SVMI	CCS
Cordoba	SACE	COR
Georgetown	SYGC	GEO
Guatemala City	MGGT	GUA
Havana	MUFH	HAV
Kingston	MKJK	KIN
La Paz	SLLP	LPB
Lima	SPLI	LIM
Managua	MNMG	MGA
Mexico City	MMMX	MEX
Montevideo	SUAA	MVD
Nassau	MYNA	NAS
Panama City	MPTO	PTY
Paramaribo	SMPB	PBM
Port-au-Prince	MTPP	PAP
Port of Spain	TTPS	POS
Quito	SEQU	UIO
Rio de Janiero	SBGL	RIO
San José	MRSJ	SJO
San Juan	TJSJ	SJU
Santiago	SCEL	SCL
Santa Domingo	MDSD	SDQ
Sao Paulo	SBSP	SAO
Tegucigalpa	MHTG	TGU

Africa and Middle East

Abidjan	DIAP	ABJ
Accra	DGAA	ACC
Addis Ababa	HAAA	ADD
Algiers	DAAA	ALG
Amman	OJAI	AMM
Baghdad	ORBS	
Bahrain	OBBI	BAH
Beirut	OLBA	BEY
Cairo	HECA	CAI
Capetown	FACT	CPT
Casablanca	GMMM	CAS
Dakar	GOOV	DKR
Damascus	OSDI	DAM
Doha	OTBD	DOH
Dubai	OMDB	DXB
Freetown	GFLL	FNA
Gabarone	FBGR	GBE
Harare	FVHA	HRE
Johannesburg	FAJS	JNB
Khartoum	HSSS	KRT
Kinshasa	FZAA	FIH
Kuwait	OKBK	KWI
Lagos	DNMM	LOS
Larnaca	LCLK	LCA
Lusaka	FLLS	LUN
Nairobi	HKJK	NBO
Riyadh	OERK	RUH
San'a	OYSN	SAH
Tehran	OIII	THR
Tel Aviv	LLBG	TLV
Tripoli	HLLT	TIP
Tunis	DTTA	TUN
Windhoek	FYHQ	WDH

Asia and Oceania

Almaty	UAAA	ALA
Auckland	NZAA	AKL
Bandar Seri Bagawan	WBSB	BWN
Bangkok	VTBD	BKK
Beijing	ZBAA	BJS
Christchurch	NZCH	CHC
Colombo	VCBI	CMB
Delhi	VIDP	DEL
Dhaka	VGFR	DAC
Hanoi	VVVV	HAN
Hong Kong	VHHH	HKG
Honolulu	PHNL	HNL
Jakarta	WIII	JKT
Kabul	OAKB	KBL
Karachi	OPKC	KHI
Kuala Lumpur	WMFC	KUL
Malé	VRMF	MLE
Manila	RPLL	MNL
Melbourne	YMML	MEL
Mumbai	VABB	BOM
Nadi	NFFN	NAN
Noumea	NWWM	NOU
Perth	YPPH	PER
Phnom Penh	VDPP	PNH
Pyongyang	ZKKK	FNJ
Seoul	RKSM	SEL
Sydney	YSSY	SYD
Singapore	WSSS	SIN
Taipei	RCTP	TPE
Tokyo	RJTT	TYO
Ulaanbaatar	ZMUB	ULN
Vientiane	VLVT	VTE
Yangon	VYYY	RGN

Glossary of Aviation Abbreviations

ADF	Automatic Direction Finding
ALPA	Airline Pilots Asscociation
APU	Auxiliary Power Unit
ASI	Air Speed Indicator
ATC	Approved Type Certificate
ATC	Air Traffic Control
ATIS	Air Traffic Information Service
BAA	British Airports Authority
BV	Bureau Veritas
CAA	Civil Aviation Authority
CAVOK	Cloud and Visibility OK
CTA	Control Area
c/n	Construction Number
DME	Distance Measuring Equipment
EFIS	Electronic Flight Instrumentation System
ELT	Emergency Locator Transmitter
ETA	Estimated Time of Arrival
ETD	Estimated Time of Departure
ETOPS	Extended-range Twin-engined Operations
FAA	Federal Aviation Administration (UK)
FAC	Forward Air Control
FADEC	Full-Authority Digital Electronic Control
FBO	Fixed Base Operator
FBW	Fly-By-Wire
FLIR	Forward-Looking Infra-Red
GA	General Aviation
GCA	Ground-Controlled Approach
GPS	Global Positioning System
HOTAS	Hands on Throttle and Stick
IATA	International Air Traffic Association
ICAO	International Civil Aviation Organisation
IFR	Instrument Flight Rules
ILS	Instrument Landing System
IMC	Instrument Meterological Conditions
INS	Inertial Navigation System
ISA	International Standard Atmosphere
JAR	Joint Airworthiness Requirements
MFD	Multi-Functional Display
MSA	Minimum Safe Altitude
MSL	Mean Sea Level
NDB	Non-Directional Radio Beacon
NM	Nautical Mile
NOTAM	Notice to Airmen
NTSB	National Transportation Safety Board (USA)
PAPI	Precision Approach Path Indicator
PAR	Precision Approach Radar
QNH	Altimeter setting above MSL

SAR	Search and Rescue	UTC	Coordinated Universal Time
SELCAL	Selective Calling		
SLAR	Sideways-Looking Airborne Radar	VASI	Visual Approach Slope Indicator
SST	Supersonic Transport	VFR	Visual Flight Rules
STC	Supplemental Type Certificate	VHF	Very High Frequency
		VMC	Visual Meteorological Conditions
STOL	Short Take-off and Landing		
		VOR	VHF Omni-directional Range
TAS	True Airspeed		
TBO	Time Between Overhauls	VSTOL	Vertical/Short Take-Off and Landing
TC	Type Certificate (USA)		
TMA	Terminal Control Area	VTOL	Vertical Take-Off and Landing
TOGW	Take-Off Gross Weight		
TORA	Take-Off Run Available		
UHF	Ultra High Frequency (radio)		